Mulehead
The Holy Grail for Moscow Mule Lovers

Copyright © JJ Resnick

The relaunch of the Moscow Copper Co. and the 75th Anniversary book Mulehead have changed the game in the cocktail world. Mulehead is the go-to resource for mule recipes for the modern-day bartender, food, and beverage director or the cocktail enthusiast imbibing at home. They delivered a one-of-a-kind copper drinking vessel to hold this iconic cocktail and followed it up with a book that keeps people sampling variations of the Moscow Mule. Cheers, America!

Art Sutley, Publisher of Bar Business Magazine

Mulehead is the perfect book for both new bartenders and the existing professionals alike. There are so many great recipes by bartenders and mixologists from all around the world along with tools, descriptions and general bar knowledge.

Phil Wills, Spirits In Motion/Bar Rescue

There's no denying when you see the copper mug what it is. I think people might be inspired to order one just by seeing one being served.

Tony Abou-Ganim, Libertine Social, Las Vegas

75
YEARS
1941 2016
ANNIVERSARY

Mulehead

The Holy Grail for Moscow Mule Lovers

75 UNIQUE VARIATIONS ON THE CLASSIC

Limited Collectors Edition 2016

JJ Resnick

True Story Publishing

Editorial

4 Tales of the Cocktail
5 Foreword
6 Introduction
8 Our Story
19 Mulehead Lifestyle
22 World Map
20 Stay Connected
223 Copper Card Program
234 Acknowledgments

Mule School

10 Copper Science
15 Caring For Your Copper
16 Basic Bar Tools
25 Vodka
95 Gin
117 Mezcal & Tequila
141 Whiskies
167 Rum
184 Sub Recipes
194 A Ginger Beer Primer
196 A Little On Limes
197 Minute Mules
218 Mini Mules
224 Copper Science Cont.
236 Glossary of Bartending Terms
238 Index

Vodka Mules

26 The Good Ship Liefde
28 Jeweled Mule
30 Maui Mule
32 Sichuan Mule
34 Mule as a Cucumber
36 One Eared Stag Mule
39 Hightide Mule
41 Stubborn Hospitality
43 Marigny Mule
45 The Ferris Mule'r
47 Sicilian Mule
48 Dragon Mule
50 The Cure to Being a Mule
52 Pineapple Ginger Mule
54 Moscow Mulada
56 The Wandering Mule
58 Duke of Orleans
60 King Palm Java Jenny
62 Grant's Mule
64 Paradise Mule
66 Summer & Smoke
68 The Pistachio Mule
70 Hair of the Mule
72 The Strand House Mule
74 Chamomule
76 El Burro Catalan
78 The Burgundian Muildier
80 The Mafia Mule
82 The Karamazov
84 Mi Vida Mule
86 Midtown Mule
88 Miso Mule
90 Blackcurrant Mule
92 The Elit Mule

Gin Mules

96 Bangkok Buckshot
98 Blossoms on Silk Road
100 Buck the French
102 Just Beet It
104 Royal Tart
106 The Cutler Family Tradition
108 Seven Sons Mule
110 Queen of Cups
112 Pedal Tone
114 Lordship Mule

Whiskey Mules

142 Dunmore Pineapple
144 Buck@ Mist
146 Farmer Elijah's Creole Mule
148 Buckaroo
150 Rocky Mountain Mule
152 Old Square Mule
154 Derby Mule
156 Smokey Donkey
158 Take Root
160 Healing Mule
162 Kicking Mule
164 Bourbon Street Mule

Mezcal & Tequila Mules

118 Mezcal Mule
120 Oaxaca Muletail
122 Aztec Mule
124 Mezican Mule
126 Diablo Mango Mule
128 Wise Oaxacan Mule
130 Hakka Mule
132 Pacific Moon
134 Tequila Hot Mule
136 Zinger Meets Mezcal
138 Oaxacan Mule

Rum Mules

168 Beet the Mule
170 Grandpa Sam
172 Haitian Mule
174 Double Barreled
176 Red-Eye Buck
178 The Carrot and Stick Approach
180 The Queen Elizabeth
182 Serpent and the Mule

About Tales of the Cocktail®

Founded in 2002, Tales of the Cocktail® has grown from a small gathering of cocktail lovers into the world's premier cocktail festival. Each year, the international spirits industry is welcomed to New Orleans for a week of seminars, tastings, networking events and much more. With 200+ annual events developed specifically for bartenders, distillers and other spirits professionals, Tales of the Cocktail® is the industry's annual meeting place for the exchanging of new ideas, products and techniques.

2016 was recognized as the Year of The Mule by TOTC and became the theme of the New Orleans based event in July. To celebrate, a competition was launched to bartenders worldwide to see who could create the most unique, mouth watering variation of the Classic Moscow Mule. Hundreds of submissions were received and in the following pages you will find many of these winning mule recipes. Please have fun exploring the pages and trying these incredible twists on the Mule. Most importantly, drink responsibly!

About the New Orleans Culinary and Cultural Preservation Society

Tales of the Cocktail® is produced by the New Orleans Culinary & Cultural Preservation Society (NOCCPS), a non-profit organization committed to supporting, promoting and growing the cocktail industry in New Orleans and around the world. In addition to offering opportunities to learn and acquire new skills through Tales of the Cocktail® events and Tales 365®, the NOCCPS invests the proceeds back into the spirits industry. Since 2008, the NOCCPS has invested more than $886,000 into programs like the Cocktail Apprentice Program, a tuition reimbursement program, the Apprentice medical aid fund, educational scholarships and a new health and wellness program for members of the hospitality industry.

WEBSITE: talesofthecocktail.com   FACEBOOK: /talesofthecocktail   TWITTER: @totc   INSTAGRAM: @tales_of_the_cocktail

Together with Tales of the Cocktail® and 75 of the world's most talented bartenders and mixologists, we are ecstatic to introduce the first edition of *Mulehead* – a beautiful Moscow Mule recipe book. With 2016 marking the 75th anniversary of the Moscow Mule, we wanted to showcase the creations of adventurous mixologists from across the globe who have shared with us their mouthwatering and unique spins on this classic cocktail.

In 1941, Grandma Sophie strolled into the Cock'n Bull, copper mugs in tow, and met her soon-to-be friends Jack Morgan and John Martin. After a few cocktails, and of course some trial and error, the Moscow Mule was born.

The seemingly simple combination of vodka, ginger beer, and lime resulted in something so much greater than the sum of its parts when mixed together in the copper mug. The biggest question people seem to ask regarding the Moscow Mule remains, "does a copper mug really make a difference, or change the taste of a Moscow Mule?" After sticking an expert scientist on the job to conduct a variety of very specific tests, we discovered the answer to be a definitive YES.

In the following pages, you'll learn the history of America's most popular craft cocktail, and read much more about the irresistible copper mugs in which they are best served. We also have 75 recipes from cocktail artists around the world for you to peruse and try out at home, as well as our very own Minute Mules™ that you can prepare for any party or gathering. Plus, you'll find many more surprises throughout the book!

On behalf of Grandma Sophie, myself (JJ Resnick), the entire team here at Moscow Copper Co., MoscowMule.com, Tales of the Cocktail®, and the 75 incredible bartenders you'll meet inside, we hope you enjoy this tribute to the 75th anniversary of this historic cocktail.

JJ Resnick

Chief Mulehead

Introduction

I would like to start by thanking my Great Grandma Sophie Berezinski, because without her, we wouldn't have the great cocktail we all know and love today. She brought us the very first Moscow Mule back in 1941, and I would like to believe that over the years we've perfected this distinctive drink.

My passion for the Moscow Mule began as a young boy. I remember sitting around the firepit in our backyard, watching the family proudly toast each other with mule after mule, as they reminisced and shared stories about Sophie. It wasn't until recently, however, that mule mugs really piqued my interest. With the mule's resurgence in popularity, I noticed the quality of the copper mugs begin to plummet – that was if you were even lucky enough to have your mule served in copper. Witnessing mules being served in faux copper, tin-lined barrel mugs, or worse yet, in glass, made me feel sorry for the patrons experiencing these inferior mules, and I felt it was disrespectful to Grandma Sophie's original copper mug and its specific design and function.

It was then that I realized, the world deserved to know how the Moscow Mule really was meant to be consumed and enjoyed. With my family history, I had the ability to provide the world with truly authentic copper mugs. I did this to help restore tradition, so that people could have the experience that a real copper mug provides, and to ensure that Grandma Sophie's reputation and legacy would live on throughout history.

When I spoke with my father about my newfound motivation to restore the mule mug, he felt it was the ideal time to hand down Grandma Sophie's original mug, the one in which she had enjoyed her very first Moscow Mule. We use the design and dimensions of Grandma Sophie's original mug as the base of the Moscow Copper Co. mugs we make today. We simply updated the size, and proportioned the mug to 16.9 ounces in order to serve the perfect modern day Moscow Mule.

I'd like to share a little more about my Great Grandma Sophie, her fascinating story, and how the Moscow Mule was born. To do this, I have to take you back to 1910. My father, Sophie's grandson, has a better understanding of this period in time, so I decided to interview him to fill in all the details. In the following pages, you will learn how Sophie went from running a copper factory with her father in Russia, to ending up in West Hollywood at the famed Cock'n Bull pub, where history – and the first Moscow Mule ever – was made.

Our Story

How It All Got Started....

If you, like millions of Americans, have recently discovered the taste explosion of the Moscow Mule, you've probably taken a moment to learn a bit about this curious cocktail. All the research in the world won't provide you with an accurate picture of this uniquely American cocktail's history though. Take a trip back in time with us, and you'll learn the hidden past of the Moscow Mule and discover just how the copper mug became such an important piece of the puzzle.

In 1941, Sophie Berezinski was a woman on a mission. She had immigrated to the United States from Russia and was carrying a heavy burden: 2,000 solid copper mugs. Sophie's father owned and operated a copper factory in Russia known as the Moscow Copper Co. Back in Russia, Sophie had created the design for the original copper mug that is now so famously linked to the Moscow Mule cocktail. Her father ran the presses that stamped out the mugs.

The one tool both Sophie and her father lacked was the slick skills of a salesman. Neither Sophie nor her father were able to sell the mugs in Russia, so the decision was made that Sophie and the mugs would journey to America. After all, it was well known that America was the land of opportunity. However, after some time, the mugs seemed destined for the scrap heap in America too. Sophie's husband Max was tired of the copper mugs cluttering the house, and issued her an ultimatum: "Find a buyer for the mugs or I'm tossing them."

Sophie couldn't bear to see the solid copper mugs she had designed and manufactured with her father end up in a landfill. She began desperately seeking out a buyer, walking door to door in Hollywood in search of a restaurant or lounge owner interested in the mugs. During one of her long days in search of a buyer for the mugs, fate intervened at the famous Cock 'n Bull pub on the Sunset Strip.

The Day History Was Made

Sophie walked into the Cock 'n Bull pub at just the right time, on the right day in 1941 to help create a cocktail America would fall in love with. John Martin had purchased the floundering Smirnoff Vodka distillery (yes, that Smirnoff) in the 1930's. Though he was successful as the head of G.F. Heublein & Brothers, a food and spirits importer that made A1 steak sauce popular, he wasn't as fortunate with vodka.

Americans had no interest in vodka. Beer, whiskey, and other cocktails ruled the roost in America at that time. Jack Morgan was in a similar bind. As owner of the Cock 'n Bull, he was trying to introduce America to his own brand of ginger beer. The two men were already good friends when they met at Morgan's pub to drown their woes. As the duo lamented their lackluster sales and sought redemption for their respective products, in walked Sophie with her solid copper mugs.

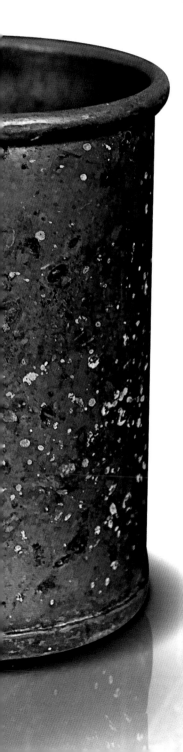

As Sophie would tell the story, the trio spent hours developing a drink that would bring together the fizzy nature of the ginger beer, the punch of the vodka, and the cold properties of copper to create the next great cocktail. After a number of taste tests and a few failed concoctions, they stumbled upon a recipe for a cocktail that would solve all their problems. The Moscow Mule was born on that day in 1941. The perfect combination of vodka and ginger beer, housed in a solid copper mug that kept the drink cold and enhanced its flavor and aroma, resulting in a cocktail that America would fawn over for the next two decades.

The Original Cock 'n Bull Pub, Hollywood, CA

Setting the Record Straight

For decades, Sophie's role in the creation of the Moscow Mule remained shrouded in mystery. Always referred to as the "third party" or "unnamed contributor," it was Sophie's solid copper mugs that gave the cocktail its distinct presentation. Today, her great grandson JJ Resnick operates the Moscow Copper Co. to provide the new generation of Moscow Mule fans with Sophie's Original Mule Mug.

When Sophie introduced John and Jack to her original solid copper mugs in 1941, they were made of 100% heavy gauge copper. The mugs had a simple, yet attractive design. The Moscow Copper Co. original mugs sold today are those same mugs reintroduced that Sophie walked into the pub with over 70 years ago.

We call our copper mule mugs "The One, The Only...The Original" for a reason. The mugs we make today at our small, family owned company are manufactured following Sophie's exacting specifications. We use the original molds from Sophie and follow her notes to the letter, including the directions for affixing the heavy gauge solid copper handle. Every other "original" mule mug on the market today is an imposter. The Moscow Copper Co. Original Mule Mug is the only one based on the original design.

Every one of our mugs comes with a lifetime guarantee. The next time you hoist a Moscow Mule, lift it in the mug its creators intended. Lift it in a Moscow Copper Co. Original Mule Mug.

Sophie Berezinski with her husband Max Berezinski

"If it wasn't for Papa Max, Sophie would have been the first American hoarder." - Mr. Resnick

Copper SCIENCE

Why is a Moscow Mule in a Copper Mug SO Damn Good?

That bright copper mug doesn't merely look good and feel authentic — it will actually make your mule stay cooler, get fizzier and taste better. But how?

We've asked an expert scientist, Brandon Larson, to perform some experiments and find out the truth. In the following pages he will break down the results to explain the real science behind pure copper, and how it interacts with the ingredients of this classic cocktail to make it truly unique.

Finally, real experiments with real results to answer age old questions regarding the necessity and benefits of using a pure copper mug. In the coming pages, we'll explore temperature, ingredient chemistry, and share the results with full graphs of the scientific experiments we conducted.

We had three major questions when it came to the unique nature of this historical drinking vessel:

1. Does the copper vessel decrease the temperature of the cocktail and does it keep it colder longer?

2. Does copper influence the taste of the cocktail?

3. Scientifically, how does the copper vessel contribute to the overall drinking experience?

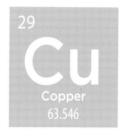

To get to the bottom of it, expert Copper Scientist Brandon Larson performed a myriad of very calculated and unbiased tests, comparing pure copper to glass and non-copper drinking vessels. His findings will leave you yearning for authenticity the next time you are served a Moscow Mule in anything but 100% pure copper.

Many will remember copper as Cu on the periodic table from high school. Copper is element 29 on the periodic table of elements, and hangs out with Silver (Ag) and Gold (Au) in Group 11 on the table, loosely known as the Coinage Metals group. Copper is a fascinating element. It can be found in nature as a pure metal, and may have been the first source of metal ever used by humans circa 8000 BC. If only early man had insight into the thermal, electrical, and chemical properties of copper — along with some advanced mixology — they might have reached for a refreshing Neolithic beverage after a long day exploring the lay of the land.

Of the common metals, copper has the highest thermal conductivity of all — almost 400 times that of glass. Glass is actually more of an insulator, so there's no conductivity there. Copper is second only to silver when it comes to electrical conductivity, which is why it is commonly used in computer components to reduce heat, and why most wires are full of copper. Copper conducts heat and electricity incredibly well — and these are two important properties that lend themselves to the titillating experience of drinking a mule from a pure copper mug.

So, what exactly makes a copper mug superior to any other vessel for drinking Moscow Mules?

The ice, vodka, ginger beer and lime are undeniably refreshing elements for a cocktail. But something truly magical happens when they meet up with good old element 29. When the ice first makes contact with the copper, heat begins to flow from the cup to the ice, as governed by the second law of thermodynamics. The contact area is small at this point, with only ice touching copper, but the vodka changes that. The vodka creates a greater contact area with the copper, and the mug rapidly begins to chill. While the vodka itself doesn't conduct electricity, because there are no free ions, when it combines with the ginger beer, the added sodium increases the electrical conductivity.

In addition to sodium, ginger beer contains various vitamins, minerals, and compounds, including potassium and some naturally occurring sulfur-based compounds. Interactions between these and the copper chemically cause an increase in carbonation, essentially making your mule fizzier on contact!

Finally, the inclusion of the lime kicks the magic — or in this case science — into high gear. The lime is the most acidic component of the mixture.

A quick refresher on the pH scale :

Neutral = 7
Base = above 7
Acid = below 7

Components of a classic Moscow Mule:

Lime juice = 2
Vodka = 4
Ginger beer = ~4
Ice = ~7.5

As the lime is stirred into the drink, copper citrate forms, and with the iron from the lime, produces a mild flavor that masks metallic tones, potentially from the ginger beer or the ice, hence enhancing the overall flavor of the mule. At this point, we have a very cold mug, one that is so thermally conductive that it will rob your hands and lips of heat as you touch them.

The cooling sensation on the skin is dramatically enhanced by the copper unlike any other material. It bites, but is enjoyable.

All the components have now been brought together, with increased carbonation, and a new sweet and strange metallic salt flavor that masks any imperfections in the flavor of the cocktail's components. As you bring the drink to the lips, there may be a small jolt, which completes the full experience only delivered via a true Moscow Mule in a pure copper mug. This is especially true for pure copper mugs, not the coated ones. Coatings dampen the experience, and you wouldn't want that now would you?

A Few Highlights To Remember...

To dive into the full science of the experiments, refer to pages 224-233.

#1: The copper mug lets your beverage get colder faster, transferring less heat into the beverage, enabling the beverage to reach its lowest possible temperature — which turns out to be one of the key contributors to the chemistry of the cocktail.

#2: Copper influences the overall taste of your mule, thanks to interactions between the metal and the salts, vitamins, and minerals found in the ingredients of a Moscow Mule. These chemical interactions also cause an increase in carbonation, amongst other exciting things to be gone into detail later in this book.

#3: As you bring the drink to your lips a wonderful aroma is unleashed. As the mug makes contact with your mouth, heat rushes from your lips into the copper, and there may even be a small jolt – the voltage from the human body meeting the fully conductive path from drink to cup to hand – which completes the full Moscow Mule experience, only possible via a pure copper mug.

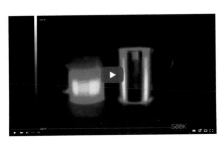

For additional details, videos, photos and more experiments, visit *MoscowMule.com/Science*

Brandon Larson | ConceiveCreateRepeat.com

Brandon Larson is one wily mechanical engineer. He holds two undergraduate degrees (Physics and Mechanical Engineering) and a Masters of Science (Mechanical Engineering). Growing up in Louisiana, he has been a scientist since childhood, whether he was blowing up stuff in the backyard, taking/breaking things apart to see how they worked, or inventing little widgets. He has worked for NASA, has managed million dollar R&D budgets for The Boeing Company, and has built a reputation as a problem solver in the areas of creativity, innovation, and design thinking within engineering and technology spaces. Today he spends most of his time with Red Bull High Performance – helping to crack the code of elite human performance through the lens of technology. The rest of his time is spent collaborating with anyone that has an interesting and fun project – be it science experiments or product development. His passions for the future reside in two areas: How agriculture will change to feed the masses and; Creating coaching tools/platforms to enable anyone to become better at what they do. He lives in Los Angeles, California with his wife, son, and yellow lab named Chowder.

Caring For Your Copper

While stunning in any state, in its shining, polished form, copper can double as decor in many spaces, or add incredible texture to a basic table setting. If you're looking to brighten up your copper mugs and barware, you'll be pleased to learn that crossing this chore off your list doesn't require a bunch of tools, a trip to the store for supplies, or even very much elbow grease. It can be tackled with as little as two ingredients, both of which you probably already have in the pantry.

We'd like to share with you a couple of proven, time-tested methods for shining up your most prized possessions.

1. The Pantry Method: Lemon and salt rank as an all-star combo for cleaning things like cutting boards, butcher block countertops and now your copper products. You likely have these two basic ingredients in the kitchen already, so why not put them to good use?

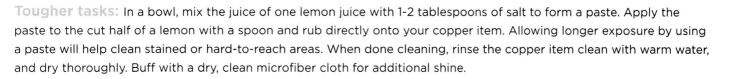

Basic cleaning: Cut a lemon in half and cover the sliced flesh with basic table salt. Rub your copper with the open-faced lemon. Use the lemon directly on the surface rather than using an applicator such as a rag or sponge. Continue to rub the surface and apply salt as needed, until tarnish is removed.

Tougher tasks: In a bowl, mix the juice of one lemon juice with 1-2 tablespoons of salt to form a paste. Apply the paste to the cut half of a lemon with a spoon and rub directly onto your copper item. Allowing longer exposure by using a paste will help clean stained or hard-to-reach areas. When done cleaning, rinse the copper item clean with warm water, and dry thoroughly. Buff with a dry, clean microfiber cloth for additional shine.

2. The Quick ands Easy Method:
Grandma Sophie's Crazy Copper Cleaner

Most people know Grandma Sophie for her part in creating the Moscow Mule, by bringing the copper mug to the party. But very few people know that she also invented a copper cleaner that she shared only with her family and very close friends. We were recently going through an old box of her belongings and came across her top-secret formula. We've been testing it in-house for the past few months, and we've decided it's just too good to not share it with the rest of the world. As we mentioned, if you just have a simple project, we suggest you go with the all natural lemon and salt method. However, for your tougher projects or if you just want to get the job done in a few seconds, go with Grandma Sophie's Crazy Copper Cleaner.

Basic Bar Tools

The bartenders who have shared their mule recipes and creations with us for this book are talented industry experts who know all the tricks of the trade. And some of those tricks involve tools. If you have a set of basic tools, they make it easier to mix an array of cocktails, both classic and contemporary. As you continue to build and add to your bar tool kit, you'll be able to expand your cocktail making repertoire, and impress even the most discerning cocktail afficionados with your mixology skills.

Here are some of the basics tools to have on hand at the home bar:

Moscow Copper Co. Mule Mugs

An essential for those beloved mules, only an authentic Moscow Copper Co. mule mug will do. Choose between original or hammered copper.

Jigger or Measuring Cup

The classic hourglass shaped jigger is a metal measuring device, usually consisting of two conical cups, one side measuring 1 ounce (aka a "pony" shot) and the other side measuring 1 and a 1/2 ounces (a "jigger").

Boston Shaker

The standard shaker used by most bartenders, the Boston features a heavy-bottomed, tempered 16 ounce glass, and a larger stainless steel cup.

Cobbler Shaker

An alternative to the aforementioned Boston Shaker, the Cobbler style is a little easier to use for home mixologists. This three part shaker features a shaker, a lid with a built-in strainer, and a cap for the lid. In some Cobblers, the lid is also a one ounce shot measure.

Julep Strainer

This spoon-shaped strainer is usually the preferred choice when straining a cocktail from a mixing glass versus a shaker or tin.

Hawthorn Strainer

The metal strainer that bartenders often use in conjunction with the Boston Shaker, to hold back ice or any loose ingredients, such as herbs, fruit or pulp. The Hawthorn features two to four prongs to keep it from slipping into the shaker, and a metal coil for a snug fit.

Tea Strainer

A small, fine mesh strainer that can be used to double-strain drinks, especially cocktails that feature fresh juices or egg whites.

Muddler / Muddling Stick

While many home bartenders make do with using a wooden spoon or its handle, a muddling stick is custom-built for the task. Various sizes are usually available, and feature a flat end that is used to gently mash fruit, sugar cubes, fresh herbs and the like to release their oils and aromas. While wooden muddlers are more traditional, stainless steel and silicone varieties are gaining popularity.

Peeler

A swivel-style vegetable peeler is ideal for cutting strips of zest from citrus fruits without getting too much of the bitter pith part of the peel. A Y-shaped peeler also works, and offers a wider blade, to cut larger sections of zest, often used for garnish.

Corkscrew / Bottle Opener

Most home bars are already equipped with the wine and bottle opening device commonly known as the " waiter's friend" — it includes a cork-screw for opening wine or any corked bottle, a bottle cap opener, and a small knife that is handy for cutting foil, wax or plastic bottle caps or wrappers.

Ice Cube Trays and Molds

A wide variety of ice trays and molds are available today. The silicon trays that make uniform cubes of ice of around 1 by 1 inch are ideal for cocktails such as a mule, while the 2 by 2 inch cubes work well for drinks served on the rocks. Find trays you like and that suit your cocktail preferences, and for the best results, always use filtered water to make your ice.

Bar Spoon

A long-handled metal spoon that is at least 10 inches in length and features a spiral handle, it is used for stirring or building drinks, either in a shaker or a glass.

Juicer or Citrus Press

A hinged citrus press large enough for lemons, limes or even smaller citrus such as tangerines is ideal for a home bar, and for cocktails that require smaller amounts of freshly squeezed citrus juice, such as our favorite — the Moscow Mule.

Zesters

A microplane style zester is ideal for finely zesting citrus fruits such as limes and lemons, and also works well for ginger, and for hard spices such as nutmeg.

Bar Towels

Small towels are any bartender's multi-purpose essential, from mopping up ice or spills, wrapping ice for crushing, or covering the top of a champagne bottle while uncorking.

Ice Bucket

When mixing drinks, it's always handy to have a bucket of fresh ice on hand, and out in the open and available to guests. To avoid handling the ice, a pair of metal tongs or a scoop are also useful, to help you or guests transfer the ice into shakers or serving glasses.

Mulehead
Lifestyle.

You might be asking yourself, "What does it mean to be a Mulehead?"

Well, it starts with one simple phrase: Truly Original.

That means being true to yourself, embracing your own originality and never settling for less. As a Mulehead, you are expected to always be the authentic version of yourself. To never hesitate to craft your own version, or to sing your own song.

As a Mulehead, you are also someone who appreciates quality, authenticity and values the history of this fine drink.

Our inner mule is passionate and adventurous. We hold nothing back and have one desire — to live life to the fullest. We never dwell on the past, we march forward with a positive outlook on the present and the future. We don't see the glass as half empty or half full, we see it as overflowing and refillable.

We enjoy the finer things in life, and we believe in the abundance principal.

Grandma Sophie was the first Mulehead. We are simply following her lead, as she embraced all of the above, and inspires us today to be the best Muleheads we can possibly be.

Muleheads, we salute you, and invite you to embrace your originality, find your inner mule and join us in enjoying the Mulehead Lifestyle!

Hey Mulehead!

We are so excited for you to begin exploring your inner mixologist by creating the 75+ unique mule variations included in the coming pages. We would also encourage you to start mixing your own concoctions after going through the book. We can't wait to see what you come up with. Please share your RECIPES & PHOTOS with us at MoscowMule.com for a chance to be featured in the next edition of *Mulehead!*

@MoscowCopper   **#moscowcopper**   **#mulehead**

Add us across social for contests, giveaways and tag us to get featured across our digital channels — and visit us at MoscowCopper.com to follow our mule blog and shop our original mugs, copper barware and more.

Subscribe to our

You Tube **channel**

to see these **mouth-watering** recipes and more!

WWW.YOUTUBE.COM/MOSCOWCOPPER

@sayward
Lake Los Carneros Park ›

@sweetnboozy

@vgillette

@laurenazline

@evakosmasflores

@punzone
The Club By Dominik Mager ›

@thristyeats
Silver Creek Valley Country Club ›

@wgno
New Orleans, Louisiana ›

@thegoodlionbar

75 recipes from around the world.

Vodka Mules

As one of the main elements of a classic Moscow Mule, vodka is a spirit close to our hearts. Vodka's origins can be found in Eastern Europe — the name stems from the Russian word for water, which is "voda." The majority of vodka is made using grains such as corn, wheat or rye, not potato, which is a common misconception. Vodka is not generally aged, and thus is a crisp, smooth, colorless liquor. In the so-called "vodka belt" countries – including Belarus, Estonia, Finland, Iceland, Latvia, Lithuania, Norway, Poland, Russia, Sweden, and Ukraine – vodka is often served chilled. Vodka's lack of a strong flavor means that it has become a popular element in many mixed drinks and cocktails, including our beloved Moscow Mule. Enjoy the following recipes, where bartenders have retained the vodka element but added other flavors and ingredients to create their own unique variation of the Moscow Mule.

The Good Ship Liefde

CREATED BY *Katy O'Donnell*

Bartender, The Nice Guy, West Hollywood, CA

INGREDIENTS

- 2 ounces Ketel One vodka
- ½ ounce lime juice
- ¾ ounce shiso ginger syrup *(Pg. 191)*
- ½ ounce filtered sake
- Sparkling cucumber juice, to top *(juice a cucumber, and charge with CO2. If you don't have a CO2 charger at home, simply combine soda water and cucumber juice at a 1:1 ratio.)*
- Citrus peel, for garnish

DIRECTIONS

Add all ingredients, except the sparkling cucumber juice, to a shaker tin. Dry shake with one cube, add ice, short shake, then strain over ice, and top with sparkling cucumber juice. Garnish with citrus peel boat.

INSPIRATION

My inspiration for this cocktail came from the desire to use sake in a mule. I wanted to use Ketel One, a Dutch vodka, so I researched the history of the Netherlands and Japan, trying to find a link between the vodka and sake, and I found a rich history. In 1598, five ships left Rotterdam loaded with trade goods heading to the far east, and the only vessel to make the daunting journey successfully was a ship called Da Liefde. Its arrival opened up trade lines between The Netherlands and Japan, paving the way for the future of the spice trade. I used the shiso leaves to incorporate the idea of trading traditional Asian goods, and I added the cucumber for its refreshing flavor, which pairs well with both sake and vodka. The drink is refreshing, and also celebrates the strong trade relations that the Dutch have with countries all around the world.

Katy **O'Donnell**

 @boozyyogi

Katy's background in live theatre makes bartending the perfect fit for her outgoing and imaginative personality. Every opportunity to make a drink is an opportunity to perform, and to create a memorable, fun and unique experience. Originally from Franklin, Massachusetts, Katy loves the creative and culturally unique city of Los Angeles, and enjoys using its endless supply of fresh ingredients in her cocktails.

Jeweled Mule

CREATED BY *Ariel Scalise*

Bartender, Grit & Grace, Pittsburgh, PA

INGREDIENTS

- 2 ounces Absolut Ruby Red vodka
- ¾ ounce John D. Taylor's Velvet Falernum
- ½ ounce lemongrass simple syrup
- ½ ounce lime juice
- ¼ ounce Crème de Violette
- 2 ounces soda water
- 3 dashes The Bitter Housewife's grapefruit bitters
- ¾ ounces muddled fresh ginger
- 1 pea sized wasabi ball

DIRECTIONS

Peel and slice three quarters of an ounce of fresh ginger. Place in tin and muddle aggressively. Add one pea-sized wasabi ball to tin, and add three dashes of The Bitter Housewife's grapefruit bitters. Add all remaining liquid ingredients to tin, add ice and thoroughly shake to combine all ingredients. Fine strain into mule mug with three one-by-one-inch ice cubes and top with soda water. Garnish with a sprig of fresh mint.

INSPIRATION

I gather my inspiration from adding tiki and Asian influences to amplify the typical mule recipe. Adding the fresh wasabi amplifies the ginger bite without loosing it. Using Absolut Ruby Red is using a quality vodka with more flavor and depth than a non-flavored vodka. I am a huge fan of lemongrass flavor so the lemongrass simple syrup really blends with the wasabi perfectly. The Crème de Violette and Falernum give the mule almost a delicate aspect to balance the kickback from the spiciness of the ginger and wasabi.

Ariel **Scalise**

@ariel.j.scalise

Ariel Scalise is an industry lifer from Pittsburgh, Pennsylvania. She started bartending in 2009, working in nightclubs, which enabled her to learn speed and basic spirit knowledge. Ariel now resides at Tender Bar + Kitchen in Pittsburgh's Lawrenceville neighborhood, where she is constantly learning and challenging herself in the art of crafting cocktails. In her personal life outside the bar, Ariel enjoys balancing the roles of wife, mom, and bartender.

Maui Mule

CREATED BY *Lexy Biller*

Bartender, Crane Ramen, Gainesville, FL

INGREDIENTS

- 1 ½ ounces Reyka vodka
- 1 egg white
- ¾ ounce pineapple-sage shrub *(Pg. 186)*
- ¾ ounce St. Germain elderflower liqueur
- Juice of 1 lime
- Barritt's ginger beer

DIRECTIONS

Combine all ingredients except the ginger beer into a shaker. Double shake and fill the mule mug with ice. Strain and top with ginger beer. Garnish with a pineapple leaf.

INSPIRATION

As a bartender I have recently been exploring using egg whites in my cocktails — I just love the texture the fluffy whites bring. So I thought incorporating that along side the bold flavors of pineapple – plus the floral component of the elderflower liqueur – would pair super well and come together for a nice a play on a Moscow Mule.

Lexy *Biller*

Lexy Biller tends bar at Crane Ramen, a hip Japanese restaurant in Gainesville, Florida that's pushing the boundaries of typical college town dining with its combination of hand-crafted ramen and innovative cocktails. Focused on seasonal and area-sourced ingredients, Lexy is the mind behind a unique selection of specialty drinks making Crane Ramen one of Gainesville's top cocktail destinations. While pursuing her degree in Digital Arts and Science at the University of Florida, she discovered an even greater interest in the art of craft cocktails. Just 22 years old, Lexy has a passion for hospitality, a keen eye for detail, and a natural and growing talent for mixology. She hopes to continue to develop her craft behind the bar, and to make a big impact on the cocktail scene.

Sichuan Mule

CREATED BY *Jane Liu*

Yuen Long, Hong Kong

INGREDIENTS

- 2 ounces Absolut vodka
- 1 ½ ounces spiced pineapple juice *(Pg. 188)*
- ½ ounce lime juice
- ½ ounce fresh ginger juice
- 1 ½ ounces ginger beer

DIRECTIONS

Combine all ingredients (except ginger beer) in a shaker, add ice, shake well and then double strain into the chilled mule mug filled with crushed ice. Slowly top up with ginger beer. Serve with Sichuan hot pot spices.

INSPIRATION

Combining the elements of a Sichuan spicy hot pot, this cocktail is a classic twist with oriental flavor. The Sichuan spicy hot pot is known for its spicy, numbing, yet fragrant flavor. I made spiced pineapple juice by heating it with hot pot spices, resulting in a smooth spicy-sweet flavor. The drink starts with the fragrance of the spices, then continues with the sweetness of the pineapple, which is then balanced by the citrusy notes of lime, and rounds out with a hint of ginger. The choice of keeping ginger beer in the recipe was made in order to enhance the drink with that lovely bubbly sensation, which also echoes with the complex spices. It keeps the original Moscow Mule's simplicity, yet creates a unique freshness with layers of spiciness.

Jane **Liu**

f /alienjane.liu 🅞 @alienjane

Jane Liu describes herself as a cocktail geek, or specifically, an alcoholic escapist with preference for beautiful drinks. Born and raised in Hong Kong, a fast-developing cocktail destination, Jane is in love with the cocktail culture in the city she calls home. She feels that there is always something more to learn about bartending, and is constantly in the pursuit of making perfect drinks. Her concept on cocktail creation — always be bold. And taste wise, she feels it is important not to be afraid of twisting modern and traditional elements.

Mule as a Cucumber

CREATED BY *Brian Prugalidad*

Assistant Bar Manager, Bracero Cocina, San Diego, CA

INGREDIENTS

- 1 ½ ounces Aylesbury Duck vodka
- ½ ounce Ancho Reyes chile liqueur
- ¾ ounce fresh lime juice
- 3/8 ounce black pepper syrup *(Pg. 187)*
- 3/8 ounce ginger syrup *(Pg. 187)*
- Dash of Peychaud's bitters
- Pinch of salt
- Two slices of English cucumber
- Fever-Tree Premium soda water

DIRECTIONS

In a shaker, muddle cucumber and add all ingredients except soda water. Take one ice cube and whip until fully integrated. Pour into a copper mule mug over fresh ice and top with Fever-Tree Premium soda water. Garnish with english cucumber slices, one coated with ground black pepper, the other coated with sea salt.

INSPIRATION

I knew I wanted to create a drink that wasn't too much of a deviation from the original mule, but still had its own identity. I also know that I wanted it to have a 'kick' of some sort, while still being a cocktail that people can enjoy more than one of in the humid New Orleans climate. After the name came to me, the rest fell into place pretty quickly and fluidly.

Brian **Prugalidad**

 /P.Dad Pours   @.pdadpoursdrinks

Brian was born and raised in San Diego, California and – and after living up and down the West Coast – is now raising his own family there. A veteran of the San Diego craft cocktail scene, Brian is proud to have been able to stand behind the stick at many notable bars: Craft & Commerce and Polite Provisions (both of which were nominated for Best High Volume Bar at Tales of the Cocktail, the latter winning in 2014), Seven Grand San Diego, Bankers Hill Bar + Restaurant, and – most recently – the James Beard-nominated Bracero Cocina. Brian absolutely loves what he does and finds himself blessed to be part of an amazing community. That sense of community is something he not only hopes can be seen and felt, but tasted in every sip of these handcrafted cocktails.

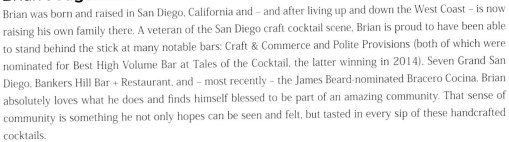

One Eared Stag Mule

CREATED BY *Mikey Kilbourne*

Beverage Director, One Eared Stag, Atlanta, GA

INGREDIENTS

- 2 ounces Reyka vodka
- ½ ounce Dolin Genepy des Alpes liqueur
- ¼ ounces lime juice
- ¼ ounce cane sugar syrup
- 2 dashes lemongrass tincture *(Pg. 187)*
- Approximately 3 ounces ginger beer *(Pg. 187)*

DIRECTIONS

Build drink in a copper mule mug, and then top with ginger beer and crushed ice. Garnish with microplaned lime zest.

INSPIRATION

The classic Moscow Mule is delicious, but I believe it lacks the depth and dimension of some of today's highly sophisticated cocktails. The addition of the Genepy liqueur adds the herbal, botanical notes that the drink was missing. Lemongrass adds a bright vegetal component that plays very well with the botanical notes of the Genepy. The homemade ginger beer brings everything together into a harmonious libation that will be the best mule you've ever tasted.

Mikey **Kilbourne**

f /mkilbourne89, /oneearedstag @mikeykilbourne, @oneearedstag

A native Atlantan, Mikey Kilbourne discovered his passion for cooking as a teenager. While his initial plan was to follow in his father's footsteps and become a doctor, the more time he spent in the kitchen, the more he realized he could not imagine having a career in any other industry. He is a graduate of the Culinary Institute of America (CIA) in Hyde Park, New York, where he received an associate's degree in Culinary Arts and ultimately graduated with a bachelor's degree in Culinary Arts Management. After CIA he returned home to Atlanta, where he was hired at Bacchanalia, and learned about hospitality in one of the region's great dining rooms. Mikey brings his passion for great ingredients and unique flavor combinations to his work behind the bar, where his culinary training is apparent in the house-made syrups, tinctures, bitters and other cocktail ingredients that ascribe to the One Eared Stag philosophy of making everything on premise from scratch. When he's not at One Eared Stag, you might find Mikey working with clients on private dinners through his company Pilot Light, a passion project that draws on his knowledge of high-level cooking, service and beverage pairing.

Hightide Mule

CREATED BY *Megan Ben*

Bartender, Tony's Saloon, Los Angeles, CA

INGREDIENTS

- 1 ½ ounces vodka
- ¾ ounce Giffard Ginger of the Indies
- ¾ ounce lime juice
- ½ ounce passion fruit syrup
- 3 dashes cardamom bitters
- ½ ounce float of Lemon Hart 151 rum

DIRECTIONS

Shake all ingredients together, except the 151 rum. Strain over fresh ice into a copper mug. Float with a half ounce dash of the 151 rum — which may be lit on fire if desired.

INSPIRATION

I love tiki and tropical flavors, so I wanted to incorporate those in to my take on the classic Moscow Mule. Fire is always fun, too!

Megan **Ben**

@TonysSaloon @meganbartendress, @TonysSaloon, @213Hospitality

Megan has been bartending for about five years, and a good portion of that time has been spent behind the bar at Tony's Saloon in the Arts District of downtown Los Angeles. If she wasn't a bartender, Megan says would choose a career in the kitchen, as she loves creating new and delicious cocktails that are fun takes on classics with a culinary twist. One of her favorite things about creating cocktails is the prep in the kitchen, coming up with new syrups, infusions and other ingredients. Megan finds her inspiration for cocktails in all kinds of places, such as 2 Chainz songs, the farmers market, and her search for how many ways she can use pamplemousse and maple syrup in cocktails.

Stubborn Hospitality

CREATED BY *Cari Hah*

Bar Manager, Big Bar at Alcove, Los Angeles, CA

INGREDIENTS

- 1 ½ ounces pineapple infused Aylesbury Duck vodka
- 3 muddled basil leaves
- ¾ ounce fresh lime juice
- East Imperial ginger beer
- Ginger foam

DIRECTIONS

Whip shake three muddled basil leaves with the pineapple-infused vodka and lime juice, and then strain into a copper mug. Add fresh ice, top with ginger foam, slap a fresh basil leaf and garnish.

INSPIRATION

I was inspired by the fresh produce I can get year round here in LA! I like the bright, slightly sweet pineapple flavor with the sharpness of the ginger. It is very aromatic as you lift the drink to take a sip. The flavors come together to create a very refreshing, quaffable cocktail that I can totally imagine myself sipping on a patio on a perfectly sunny Los Angeles day.

Cari **Hah**

 @carisunnie

Cari Hah is the Bar Manager at Alcove's Big Bar in Los Angeles. She has been a bartender, consultant, and brand representative for many years, and has worked her craft at LA area bars including The Varnish, Blue Whale, Izakaya Fu-ga, Cole's, Neat, Three Clubs and Clifton's Cafeteria. She has competed in and won several competitions: G'vine Gin global competition (2012), Jameson Black Barrel competition (2015), and Speedrack (regional finalist contender 2013, 2015). She is known as a cheerleader for the LA bartending community, and as a tiger mom to her staff. If she's not behind the bar, Cari is probably eating KitKats and hanging out with her friends and family, and her two-pound Maltese, Noni.

Marigny Mule

CREATED BY *Brian Christie*

Assistant Food & Beverage Manager, Ritz-Carlton New Orleans, New Orleans, LA

INGREDIENTS

- 1 ounce Grey Goose vodka
- ½ ounce Deep Eddy grapefruit vodka
- ½ ounce tarragon-lime syrup *(Pg. 186)*
- 2 ounces Gosling's ginger beer
- 1 sprig of tarragon, for garnish
- 1 grapefruit wedge, for garnish

DIRECTIONS

In a copper mug, add ice, the two vodkas and the tarragon-lime simple syrup. Fill the drink with Gosling's ginger beer. Smack a tarragon sprig to release the flavor and oils into the drink, and add a grapefruit wedge onto the rim of the mug.

INSPIRATION

The inspiration behind this cocktail is walking around the Marigny neighborhood of New Orleans, and needing a light citrus drink to cool off in the summertime. The flavors of grapefruit and tarragon pair very well and add a nice element to the traditional Moscow Mule.

Brian **Christie**

 @bchris310

Brian Christie is a graduate of Penn State University and has been in the hospitality industry for over nine years. He previously worked at the Ritz-Carlton Naples, where he supervised the bar that was renovated and rebranded into Dusk Sushi Bar. Brian focused on fresh cocktails with an Asian twist to pair with the sushi. He currently works as the Assistant Food and Beverage Manager at the Ritz-Carlton New Orleans, where he oversees the wine program and assists with the cocktail menu.

The Ferris Mule'r

CREATED BY Gary Wayne Burleson Jr.
Bartender, Dogwood Cocktail Cabin, Bend, OR

INGREDIENTS
- 2 ounces vodka
- 3 lime slices
- 5 mint leaves and 1 sprig
- 2 nickel sized slices of peeled ginger
- 5 ounces Coco Lopez Cream of Coconut
- Pinch of salt
- 1 thick orange slice
- Gosling's ginger beer, to top
- Soda water, to top

DIRECTIONS
First muddle the limes, mint, and ginger with ice. Then add a little more ice, the vodka, salt, and the Coco Lopez. Shake it, but don't fake it. Dump it, dirty Southern style (without straining) into the copper mug. Top with half Gosling's ginger beer and half soda water. Garnish with a fat orange slice and a lively sprig of mint. Enjoy with this quote in mind: "Life moves pretty fast. If you don't stop and look around once in a while, you could miss it." –Ferris Bueller

INSPIRATION
July is arguably the busiest month for the service industry. Everywhere is super busy, tourists are climbing in the windows with fanny packs stuffed full of vacation cash, and new summer hires are running around like chickens with their heads cut off. This is not a good time to take time off — but it is the BEST time to take time off! Inspired, of course, by the movie and titular character *Ferris Bueller's Day Off*, the Ferris Mule-er is all about slipping off to play hooky and letting the world grind on without you for a few days. It has been designed for unapologetic day drinking, and is best served aboard a parade float.

Gary Wayne **Burleson Jr.**

@snowbirdsmargaritatruck, @yesthegaryshow

Born in West Virginia and raised in Asheville, North Carolina, Gary always wanted to be a bartender, even as a kid. He has since become something of a bohemian, traveling across the country, tending bar from coast to coast. He first fell in love with the job of bartending in Waikiki, but learned his chops in San Francisco, and has continued bartending ever since. He's always collecting bar books and gadgets, and is continuously learning and exploring new things. Gary's favorite part of bartending is making people laugh and putting on a show. He can currently be found behind the bar at the Dogwood Cocktail Cabin in beautiful, downtown Bend, Oregon. Gary also owns the Snowbirds Margarita Truck in Central Oregon, and plans to open his own bar someday.

Sicilian Mule

CREATED BY *Carlos Ruiz*

Head Bartender, Crystal Springs Resort, Hamburg, NJ

INGREDIENTS

- 1 ounce Aylesbury Duck vodka
- 1 ounce Amaro Averna
- ¾ ounce fresh lime juice
- ¾ ounce Domaine De Canton
- ½ ounce simple syrup *(2:1 ratio)*
- 2 dashes Bittermens Hellfire Bitters
- 2 ounces club soda
- Fresh mint, for garnish

DIRECTIONS

In a cocktail shaker add all ingredients, except the club soda. Shake with ice and double strain into a copper mug filled with a 2-inch x 2-inch ice cube, and top off with the club soda. Garnish with a nice bouquet of fresh mint.

INSPIRATION

My inspiration was the original Moscow Mule — it is such a refreshing cocktail that has some nice heat to it. I used Averna because of the nice spice qualities, and the texture that it has, I thought it would bring another layer of flavor and mouthfeel to my cocktail. I also love to make low alcohol content cocktails — I feel like people enjoy them better because they can try more in one sitting.

Carlos **Ruiz**

f Carlos Fabricio Ruiz ⓘ 👻 @cocktailsbyc

Carlos Ruiz, one of most dynamic young mixology talents in the US today, oversees the cocktail program at Crystal Springs Resort's restaurants and bars. A native of Lima, Peru, Carlos came to the United States at the age of eight and has worked in the restaurant industry since he was fourteen. For a short time, Carlos studied software engineering in college, before deciding that bartending would be a more fulfilling career path. His career behind the bar began at the relaunched Ryland Inn, where he learned the basics from renowned mixologist Christopher James. He then moved on to develop the bar program at Washington House in Basking Ridge, and then Agricola in Princeton, turning the acclaimed farm to table restaurant into one of the state's top cocktail destinations. At just 24, Carlos has quickly become one of the top mixologists in New Jersey, having won numerous cocktail competitions, including first place in the New Jersey Restaurant & Hospitality Association's 2015 "Mixologist of the Year" competition, 1st place in the 2016 Iron Shaker Cocktail Competition, and many more.

Dragon Mule

CREATED BY *Janis Carlson*

Bartender, 33°North Lobby Bar, Monach Beach Resort, Dana Point, CA

INGREDIENTS

- 1 ½ ounces Ketel One Oranje
- 3 dashes rhubarb bitters
- 4 large pieces of fresh dragon fruit
- 3 ounces ginger beer
- ¾ ounce Domaine de Canton ginger liqueur
- ¾ ounce fresh squeezed lime juice
- 1 fresh peel of orange
- Blend of cayenne pepper and candied ginger for copper mug rim

DIRECTIONS

Muddle four large pieces of dragon fruit in shaker tin. Add Ketel One Oranje, rhubarb bitters and ice. Shake vigorously and strain into a copper mule mug filled with ice. Top with ginger beer and gently stir to blend all ingredients. Finish with a freshly peeled orange twist, then garnish with a slice of dragon fruit and cayenne/candied ginger on the rim.

INSPIRATION

The Dragon Mule is a twist on the Dutch Mule, and combines the flavors of fresh, bright dragon fruit, orange, rhubarb, and ginger. All of these flavors blend beautifully together. Dragon fruit is a mildly sweet, yet exotic fruit, so the sharpness of the ginger and rhubarb add a nice contrast. To bring even more fire to the Dragon Mule, a mixture of cayenne pepper and candied ginger on the rim of the copper mug brings a pleasantly surprising spice to the cocktail, which lingers on your palate as you enjoy this refreshing drink.

Janis **Carlson**

Janis Carlson lives in Dana Point, California and bartends at the 33N Lobby Bar, inside the exquisite Monarch Beach Resort. Her mixology career began when she lived in Maui and quickly learned how to craft the perfect Mai Tai. Her knowledge and interest in tropical flavors and ingredients has often inspired her recipes, even now that she lives off the islands of Hawaii. Many of what Janis dubs her "coastal cocktail" creations have received wide recognition and praise.

 @moanamixology

Photography By: Margaret Pattillo mpattillophotography.co

The Cure to Being a Mule

CREATED BY *Moses Laboy*
Consulting Operations and Beverage Director, Bottle & Bine, New York, NY

INGREDIENTS

- 2 ounces Ketel One vodka
- 1 1/2 ounces Fever-Tree seltzer water
- 1 ounce turmeric/galangal sweetener *(Pg. 190)*
- 1/2 ounce fresh lime juice
- 3 dashes Angostura bitters
- Fired Cinnamon Tincture spritz *(Pg. 190)*
- Lime wheel, for garnish

DIRECTIONS

Build all ingredients over ice in a copper mug, except the cinnamon tincture. Finish by spritzing the cinnamon tincture onto a lit match over the cocktail, to really bring out the cinnamon essence. Just don't burn your fingers! Then garnish with a lime wheel, and enjoy.

INSPIRATION

My inspiration in developing this cocktail was the classic Moscow Mule. I wanted to elevate this classic drink, while still keeping its basic flavors intact. With that in mind, I used galangal (Indian ginger) and turmeric, a species of ginger, to really bring in that spicy, fresh ginger flavor. I then balanced the cocktail with fresh lime juice for acidity, Angostura for bitters and a high quality seltzer water for effervescence.

Moses **Laboy**

 @moelabNYC @Mlaboy44

Moses Laboy is the creative cocktail mind behind several bars and eateries throughout New York City. He has been credited as one of the pioneers who brought the cocktail scene back to Harlem, via his hand in the creation of the beverage program at celebrity Chef Marcus Samuelsson's Harlem hotspots — Red Rooster and Ginny's Supper Club. A born and bred native of New York City's Spanish Harlem, Moses Laboy started his restaurant career in 1992 as a server assistant, and quickly moved up the ranks to server, head bartender and management. Moses has enjoyed success consulting on beverage programs for celebrity chefs such as Marcus Samuelsson (Red Rooster, Harlem), Elizabeth Falkner (Krescendo, Brooklyn), Annie Wayt (202 in Chelsea Market), Alex Urena (Pamplona), and restaurateur Donatella Arpaia (Donatella & D Bar). He has also had the honor of creating and serving cocktails to two U.S. Presidents — President Barack Obama and former President Bill Clinton. Moses was nominated as a top ten NYC mixologist by TimeOut New York in 2015, was published in the 75th anniversary edition of the *Mr. Boston Official Bartender's Guide*, and was published in Gary Reagan's 101 best cocktails of the year for three consecutive years (2012-2014). He has enjoyed much media attention, including being featured as an Iconoclast bartender on the Sundance channel, featured on FOX & Fox Latino, The Wendy Williams Show, and he was also featured in the cocktail culture documentary Hey Bartender. Moses is currently Consulting Operations and Beverage Director at New York's Bottle & Bine, and is a member of the Court of Master Sommeliers.

Pineapple Ginger Mule

CREATED BY *Brian Weber*

Bartender, Tuxedo Club, Tuxedo Park, NY

INGREDIENTS

- 1 ½ ounces Reyka vodka
- ½ ounce Grand Marnier
- ½ ounce fresh lime juice
- ½ ounce pineapple juice
- Dash Angostura bitters
- Dash salt
- 2 ounces Gosling's ginger beer

DIRECTIONS

Shake all ingredients, except the ginger beer, with ice. Add ginger beer to the shaker. Strain into a copper mule cup filled with fresh ice. Garnish with a slice of lime and grated fresh ginger on top of the drink.

INSPIRATION

Ginger and pineapple go really beautifully together! This is a mule with a hint of tiki inspiration. I think this drink could be made in any bar, anywhere! Would freshly made pineapple juice be awesome in this drink? Absolutely! But I used canned and it was still a great drink. Obscure ingredients are interesting and original, but I prefer finding approachable cocktail recipes that make people think, "Wow that's cool! I could whip that up that the bar tonight!" No special syrups, infusions or obscure spirits required.

Brian **Weber** /sir.brianweber, /bartenderjourneypodcast  @BarKeepTips @BartenderJourney

Brian Weber is a professional bartender at the prestigious Tuxedo Club, a private club in Tuxedo Park, New York, which was established in 1886. His first job was as a dishwasher in a local restaurant at age 14. He worked through every position from line cook, to server, bartender, manager, and eventually head chef of a Manhattan restaurant by the age of 23. After almost a decade in the restaurant industry, Brian went to live in Hawaii for a few months, and decided to go back to school in NYC for his other great passion: audio production. In 2008, when the economy went haywire, the recording studio where Brian worked for many years went out of business. He worked as freelance audio engineer, but also returned to bartending, part-time, after a long absence. He fell back in love with the hospitality industry and bartending in particular. Founder and producer of the Bartender Journey podcast, Brian has interviewed many of the most influential personalities in the bar industry.

Moscow Mulada

CREATED BY Hamei Hamedi

Bartender & Owner, Cafe Venezuela, Berkeley, CA

INGREDIENTS

- 1 ¾ ounces New Amsterdam vodka
- ¼ ounce Rum Haven coconut rum
- ½ ounce fresh muddled pineapple
- ¼ ounce fresh lime juice
- 2 ounces Fever-Tree ginger beer
- 4 drops of kava extract

DIRECTIONS

Muddle the pineapple, or give it a quick spin in a blender before adding it to the shaker tin. In the tin with the pineapple, add ice, followed by the vodka, coconut rum and lime juice. Shake briefly and pour into copper mug. Top off with ice and Fever-Tree ginger beer. Add four drops of kava extract, from a medicine dropper. Garnish with a slice of pineapple and lime. Salud!

INSPIRATION

The inspiration for the Moscow Mulada came from my teacher friend Alex. She had just had a rough week, and wanted something extra special to relax. I had just picked up the kava extract and suggested we try throwing a few drops in a new cocktail. After several trials we settled on the cocktail you see today. The coconut rum and the kava conjure thoughts of tropical vacations suitable for any time of the year.

Hamei **Hamedi**

f /thecafev @cafevberk

Hamei Hamedi is the owner operator at Cafe Venezuela in Berkeley. A Bay Area native, Hamei has spent his career making award-wining wines in California, New Zealand and Oregon, as well as award-wining food in his kitchen. However, Hamei finds the most joy behind the bar, creating cocktails for his friends and patrons. He enjoys being able to mix up custom cocktails for everybody that walks through the doors of Cafe Venezuela.

The Wandering Mule

CREATED BY *Joshua Suchan*

Proprietor at Ice and Alchemy, Bar Design and Beverage Program Consulting, Los Angeles, CA

INGREDIENTS

- 2 ounces dried hibiscus bud infused vodka *(Pg. 191)*
- 1/4 ounce Giffard Vanille de Madagascar
- 1/2 ounce lemon juice
- 2 dashes orange bitters
- Ginger beer
- Fresh mint and lemon wedge, for garnish

DIRECTIONS

In a shaker, combine all ingredients except the ginger beer. Shake and strain into a copper mug filled with cubed ice. Top up the mug with ginger beer. Garnish with a lemon wedge and a bouquet of fresh mint.

INSPIRATION

I have always appreciated the simplicity of the Moscow Mule. It's rise to popularity, both in the 1940s and again today, can be contributed to its combination of straightforward ingredients. When creating my mules, I like to find engaging flavor affinities while maintaining the simplicity of the original recipe. The goal is to intrigue and refresh any palate, ranging from novice to advanced. The Wandering Mule satisfies all of these elements and also brings a vivid red color to the table.

Joshua **Suchan**

_ice_and_alchemy

Bartending became Joshua's creative outlet when the housing collapse of 2008 essentially made his freshly-printed architecture degree all but useless. Fortunately, much of the design process transcends job types, and he began looking at cocktails as opportunities to artistically express concepts. After living in Portland, Oregon and having worked with some very talented people, including one of his mentors and biggest inspirations, Jeffrey Morgenthaler, Joshua and his wife moved down to Los Angeles in 2015. There, he founded a company called Ice and Alchemy, where he consults on bar design and develops bar programs for restaurants and chefs. He can also be found behind the stick at his newest project, Skylight Gardens in LA's Westwood neighborhood.

Duke of Orleans

CREATED BY *Robyn Wilkie*

Bartender, 7 Tales, London, England

INGREDIENTS

- 1 ½ ounces Aylesbury Duck vodka
- 1 ½ ounces ginger and pineapple shrub *(Pg. 185)*
- 1/3 ounce fresh lime juice
- 1 dash Peychaud bitters
- 2 ounces soda water
- Sprig of lemon verbena, for garnish

DIRECTIONS

To build the drink, add all ingredients except the soda water to a copper mug. Add ice cubes and gently stir. Top off with soda water, and add more ice to fill the mug. Garnish with lemon verbena.

INSPIRATION

I wanted to create a simple and replicable serve that stayed true to the roots of a classic mule, and remain a refreshing and moreish cocktail. I was inspired not only by the growing trend of the use of shrubs in cocktails in London, but I also wanted to make a drink that bartenders (and the industry) would love, whilst also incorporating some of New Orleans' history. Ginger and pineapple are a classic flavor pairing, and were the perfect match for this shrub. The pineapple adds a subtle fruitiness to the drink, balancing the spiciness of the ginger. The Peychaud bitters nicely marry the spicy and fruity flavors. The name comes from the man for which the city of New Orleans is named after.

Robyn **Wilkie**

Originally from New York, Robyn Wilkie started bartending in London three years ago, after graduating from the University of Arts with a degree in Fashion Public Relations. Since starting her career at the London Cocktail Club, she has gone on to work at many of London's most esteemed cocktail bars. Most recently she has joined the Social Company to open 7 Tales, the bar accompanying Chef Jason Atherton's most recent restaurant opening, Sosharu.

King Palm Java Jenny

CREATED BY *Joy Richard*

Bar Mash, Charleston, SC

INGREDIENTS

- 2 ounces Karlsson's vodka
- ¾ ounce ginger-coconut shrub *(Pg. 186)*
- ½ ounce Kahlua
- 2 ounces Barritt's ginger beer
- Coffee bean, pineapple leaves and lime swath, for garnish

DIRECTIONS

Combine vodka, Kahlua, and the shrub in a mixing tin. Add ice and shake. Strain into a copper mug. Add the ginger beer, then fill with crushed ice. To garnish, grate a coffee bean over the top of the crushed ice, place a lime swath twisted into a corkscrew on top, and insert three pineapple leaves vertically, in a fan formation.

INSPIRATION

This drink has an island influence, inspired by my move from Boston to Charleston, South Carolina. I get to enjoy lovely tropical weather for much of the year, and who doesn't want a tropical cocktail to enjoy while sitting back and relaxing on the beach in the sun or under the shade of a palm tree swaying in the breeze. I love how coffee and coconut play together as flavors, and ginger seemed a natural addition to this combination — I aspired to use its sharp spiciness to balance the sweetness and add richness of this cocktail.

Joy **Richard**

f /joy.richard.58   @joyrichard

With over 20 years of restaurant experience, Joy Richard has spent more than 12 of those years behind the bar, and over 14 years managing bars in Boston, Massachusetts. In 2007, Richard helped found the Boston chapter of Ladies United for the Preservation of Endangered Cocktails (LUPEC), a classic cocktail society dedicated to the "raising, breeding, and releasing of nearly extinct cocktails into the wild." More than a social networking organization, LUPEC Boston has raised over $40,000 for local women's charities since its inception. In October of 2010, as the Beverage Director of the Franklin Restaurant Group, Richard took her passion for great cocktails, spirits, and especially whiskey, to a new level when she opened The Citizen Public House in Boston's Fenway neighborhood, curating a list of over 200 whiskeys from around the globe. In September 2015, Joy Richard relocated to Charleston, South Carolina, and accepted a position at Bar Mash in the historic Cigar Factory building. Bar Mash boasts the largest collection of American whiskies in Charleston, as well as a creative and innovative craft cocktail program.

Grant's Mule

CREATED BY Anthony DeSerio

Senior Cocktail Correspondent, Faith Middleton Food Schmooze WNPR, New Haven, CT

INGREDIENTS

- 1 ounce Reyka vodka
- ¾ ounce Montelobos mezcal
- ½ ounce wild hibiscus tea syrup *(Pg. 185)*
- 1 ounce Barrow's Intense Ginger Liqueur
- Juice of ½ a fresh lemon
- Fever-Tree club soda
- Edible hibiscus flower, for garnish

DIRECTIONS

Squeeze the lemon into a copper mug, and drop in the rind. Fill mug with ice, combine all ingredients, except the club soda, in a shaker tin and add ice. Shake and double strain into the iced filled copper mug. Top with Fever-Tree club soda, and garnish with an edible hibiscus flower, from the Wild Hibiscus Flower Company.

INSPIRATION

I was inspired by two amazing women in the industry, whose products I stand behind. Charlotte Voisey who taught me the value of flavors in the spirits we use. And Jocelyn from the Wild Hibiscus Flower Company, who makes amazing products and is as exciting and effervescent as this cocktail.

Anthony **DeSerio**

f /anthony.deserio.3, /adeserio72

Anthony DeSerio, one of Connecticut's "Geeky Bartenders," is at heart a modest guy who really, really likes cocktails, the spirits that they're made of, and the history behind them. Anthony began his career behind the stick about 20 years ago, armed with nothing but a copy of Gary "Gaz" Regan's *Bartender's Bible* and the idea of how cool it would be to work behind a bar. From his first job as an on call banquet bartender for a well-known Connecticut based company, he worked his way up to bar manager. He stayed with this company for a decade, honing his skills and being mentored by Kim Snow, a James Beard award-winning chef, baker and chocolatier. Anthony moved on to spend seven years as a bar manager/beverage director and GM for the Coastal Gourmet Group, during which time he joined the Connecticut chapter of the US Bartender's Guild, where in time he would become Secretary and then acting President. With the USBG, he went on to be a finalist in many competitions and develop relationships with several spirit brands. He has had his cocktail recipes featured in several magazines and books, and can be heard on Faith Middleton's radio show Food Schmooze on WNPR in New England and online. Constantly learned and creating, Anthony now works as a judge on several world class cocktail competitions, and can currently be found behind the bar at the Ideal Tavern in Southington, CT.

Paradise Mule

CREATED BY Shane McKnight

Craft on Draft Cocktails and Top Hat Provisions, San Francisco, CA

INGREDIENTS

- 1 ½ ounces Ketel One vodka
- 1 ounce Top Hat Craft ginger beer concentrate
- 4 ounces club soda
- 2 dashes Paradise Bitters *(Pg. 188)*
- 1 large wedge of sliced lime and star anise, for garnish

DIRECTIONS

Fill a copper mug with ice, then build the mule with all ingredients, except the club soda. Top off with the club soda, then finish with a wedge of freshly sliced lime and two dashes of Paradise Bitters. Garnish with star anise.

INSPIRATION

The Paradise Mule was created because it is the epitome of a refreshing cocktail. It quickly became the most popular Craft on Draft cocktail at sporting events and music festivals across the country, including the NFL Superbowl, Coachella, Outside Lands in San Francisco, Bottlerock in Napa, and Panorama in New York. Craft on Draft cocktail technology is the science of batching and delivering world-class cocktails. Craft on Draft use a versatile ginger base called Top Hat Craft Ginger Beer Concentrate, along with vodka and filtered water, to carbonate kegs of perfect Paradise Mule. Visit Tophatprovisions.com to find the bars, restaurants and stadiums that serve the Paradise Mule on draft — or use the recipe above to craft them at home.

Shane **McKnight**

Shane McKnight, founder of Top Hat Provisions, has been a passionate bartender since 1997, a curator of craft cocktail programs since 2001, a member of the San Francisco Chapter of the United States Bartenders Guild since 2004, the National Beverage Director of Best Beverage Catering, a Craft on Draft cocktail engineer since 2010, the founder and president of Top Hat Provisions and a humble teacher of Craft on Draft cocktail technology classes all over the United States since June of 2015.

Summer & Smoke

CREATED BY *Scott Kunkler*

Bartender, The Loft, Montage Laguna Beach, CA

INGREDIENTS

- 1 ½ ounces Ketel One vodka, basil infused (Basil Fast Fusion/iSi) *(Pg. 189)*
- ½ ounce fresh lime juice
- 2 ounces smoked peach nectar *(Pg. 189)*
- 1 ½ ounces Q ginger beer
- Grilled white peaches and fresh basil, for garnish

DIRECTIONS

Combine basil infused vodka, fresh lime juice, and peach nectar with a half scoop of ice. Shake vigorously for five seconds then strain into a copper mug, three-quarters filled with cubed ice. Top with Q ginger beer. Finish by layering a ¼ scoop of crushed ice on top and garnishing with grilled white peaches and fresh basil.

INSPIRATION

There are two correlations behind the name. The first is obvious — on the nose, peaches, basil and smoke ring throughout, making one's mind drift to thoughts of summertime. The second is the Tennessee Williams play of the same name, *Summer and Smoke*, which involves the sensual and spiritual evolution of a minister's daughter as she blossoms into a woman. Our intent was to mirror this same journey with the cocktail. While staying true to the core ingredients, we simply allowed the mule to evolve.

Scott **Kunkler**

 /MontageLagunaBeach   @MontageLaguna

Scott began his career as a bartender in 1991. He has had 25 years in the hospitality industry, opening bars and training bartenders in three different countries. His varied experience, from TGIF in the early nineties to ultra lounges and high-volume nightclubs in the Bay Area, has greatly improved his skills and contributed to his core knowledge of bar showmanship. Working in Las Vegas taught Scott the importance of speed while maintaining precision, and kept him on his toes at all times. Upon arriving at Montage Laguna Beach, Scott was thrown into a change of pace as he embraced a new level of service. With a strong and ever-evolving cocktail program, Scott is challenged daily and has learned the most important aspect of creating a memorable cocktail is proof of product sourcing.

The Pistachio Mule

CREATED BY Jason LaGarenne

Bartender, Lazy Point, New York, NY

INGREDIENTS

- 2 ounces pistachio infused vodka *(Pg. 191)*
- 1 ounce simple syrup
- ¾ ounce fresh lime juice
- ½ ounce fresh ginger juice
- Ginger ale, to top (optional)

DIRECTIONS

Add all ingredients to shaker with ice and shake vigorously. Smile! Strain into a copper cup filled with fresh ice. Top with a splash of ginger ale (optional) and garnish with a lime wedge or a lime twist. Cheers!

INSPIRATION

Inspiration for the Pistachio Mule struck one winter while I was sitting in front of a roaring fire, eating a massive bowl of pistachios and watching the New York Rangers play hockey. Between periods, a commercial for pistachios featuring the Korean rapper Psy came on, and I wondered to myself why there were no pistachio flavored vodkas, since they've attempted virtually every other flavor. I immediately got to work experimenting with making my own pistachio vodka. It ended up being the key ingredient in an extremely interesting and refreshing variation of the classic Moscow Mule, and eventually became our top selling cocktail.

Jason **LaGarenne**

   @lazypointnyc

Jason LaGarenne, born in Brooklyn and raised in East Hampton, has over 15 years of experience in the nightlife and hospitality industry. He began his career in the Hamptons back in 2002, and has since worked in several of New York City's hottest nightclubs and bars. Although LaGarenne has operated venues for the last eight years, he still considers himself a barman at heart, and continues to work behind the bar and develop cocktails as often as possible. As a managing partner at Lazy Point — a beach themed cocktail bar in Manhattan's Hudson Square neighborhood — he hopes to bring his passion for service and spirits to a new audience, as well as bringing a relaxed vibe to downtown New York City.

Photography by: Arthur Kna

Hair of the Mule

CREATED BY *Kevin Goleman*

Bar Manager, Troon Golf, Silver Creek Valley Country Club, San Jose, CA

INGREDIENTS

- 1 ½ ounces vodka
- ¼ lemon
- 1 teaspoon honey
- 1 pinch cayenne pepper
- 3-5 pieces pickled ginger
- Ginger beer, to top

DIRECTIONS

Muddle all ingredients in a copper mug, add ice and fill with ginger beer. Stir the cocktail, to allow the goodness from the bottom to reach the top. Trust the bartender, this helps.

INSPIRATION

The Hair of the Mule came about, as most great inventions do, as the product of necessity. After an evening spent enjoying traditional mules with friends during our annual hacker's cup golf tournament, I woke up for an early morning tee time needing a little something to "help the golf swing." To the leftover Stoli and ginger beer, I added some of the lemon, cayenne and ginger drink my wife had packed for me. The final touch was the leftover honey from the room service breakfast. And with that, the Hair of the Mule was born. While it in no way helped my golf game (not much does) it did provide a refreshing alternative to a Bloody Mary. This is also a great cocktail to loosen up before the weekend round of golf during the summer, or to enjoy with fellow fans at an early season tailgate party.

Kevin **Goleman**

@thebbtc @SilverCreekValleyCC

Kevin started his journey in the bar industry at the legendary watering hole CarPool in Arlington, Virginia, and has since seen stops on both coasts. He has spent the last eight years making members happy as the Bar Manager at Silver Creek Valley Country Club in the heart of the Silicon Valley. When not making libations, Kevin enjoys a late afternoon round of golf, listening to a ballgame on the radio and attempting to keep his beautiful wife Jes happy (which we are told is exactly 94.7% of the time).

The Strand House Mule

CREATED BY *Levi Lupercio*

Director of Wine & Cocktail Program, The Strand House, Manhattan Beach, CA

INGREDIENTS

- 1 ½ ounces Ketel One Oranje
- ½ ounce lime
- 3 dashes of Bar Keep apple bitters
- Splash of ginger ale
- Ginger beer, to top
- Granny Smith apples, mint and lime, for garnish

DIRECTIONS

Gently shake vodka, lime, ginger ale, ginger beer and apple bitters in a cocktail shaker. Pour into a copper mug, and garnish with apples, mint and lime!

INSPIRATION

The Strand House Moscow Mule is a modern approach to this classic cocktail. We add apple bitters and an apple garnish for a crisp new take on this refreshing drink. Enjoy!

Levi **Lupercio**

@strandhousemb, @strandbarmb

Born and raised in Central California, Levi has been at the forefront of the cocktail scene since he arrived in Los Angeles in 1999. He previously ran the beverage program at the acclaimed Trump National Golf Course in Rancho Palos Verdes, and has been running the wine and cocktail program at The Strand House since its conception. With over 25 years of hospitality experience, Levi's passion is creating seasonal and artisanal cocktails and finding unique wines to enhance The Strand House menu. When he's not behind the bar, you can find Levi golfing, traveling and going to shows.

Chamomule

CREATED BY *Cesar G. Perez II*

Bartender, Trade Craft Coffee & Cocktails, El Paso, TX

INGREDIENTS

- 1 ½ ounces Reyka vodka
- ½ ounce fresh lemon juice
- ½ ounce light chamomile syrup *(Pg. 185)*
- 10 drops of 18.21 chamomile bitters
- Atomizer/spritzer of 18.21 ginger lemon tincture
- ¾ ounce Gosling's ginger beer

DIRECTIONS

Shake and strain first four ingredients over an iced mule cup. Top with Gosling's ginger beer, and spritz the top of the cocktail with 18.21 Ginger Lemon tincture for an added aroma. Garnish with a lemon flower *(Pg. 185)* and serve.

INSPIRATION

Springtime in the borderland. Chamomile tea is used as much more than as a base for the widely popular Sleepy-Time tea. I've grown fond of all the individual flavors present in my cocktail, and I worked hard to make a great marriage between them. I believe this is a great riff on the mule, and I love that it is a drink that can be enjoyed year round.

Cesar G. **Perez II**

f /redwolf56 @Redwolf56

Born and raised in a West Texas border town, Cesar pulls a major influence for his cocktails from his surrounding environment. Having worked in the first entirely classic cocktail bar in El Paso, this bearded barman is able to concoct and play with classic recipes to make them fit modern trends. If he's not behind a bar or developing menus across the city, you can spot him jumping around on stilts or performing with fire.

El Burro Catalan

CREATED BY *Angel Teta*

Bar Manager, Ataula, Portland, OR

INGREDIENTS

- 1 ¾ ounces Absolut Elyx
- ¾ ounce Cigarrera Manzanilla sherry
- ¼ ounce Starvation Alley Farms cold pressed cranberry juice
- ¼ ounce natural cane sugar simple syrup *(1:1 ratio)*
- ¼ ounce lemon juice
- 2 dashes Angostura bitters
- 1 ¾ ounces Fever-Tree ginger beer

DIRECTIONS

Shake all ingredients together, except the ginger beer, then double strain into a copper mug. Add the ginger beer, and top with pebble ice. Garnish with two short stir straws and a manicured lemon peel wrapped around four skewered, dried cranberries.

INSPIRATION

Every fine drinking establishment needs a Moscow Mule these days, be it a dive bar or a proper restaurant bar. I found that adding sherry dried the ginger beer out quite nicely, and added a slight salinity that makes you want to snack on something. This was a perfect fit for my program, as we are a Catalan inspired tapas spot with incredible food. The cranberry juice I use is Starvation Alley Farms, an 100% organic cold pressed product that has such a vibrant flavor, it makes for a fantastic mule variation.

Angel **Teta**

 f /angels.envypdx @ifellasleeplikethis

Florida native Angel Teta loves to drink and mix up all of the things, be it a chilled glass of sherry or a fine Kentucky bourbon. She often finds herself competing and volunteering for cocktail weeks across the country, but she is most happy behind the stick with her Ataula familia in Portland, Oregon, the city she's called home for the last 10 years. The hospitality industry has always been very close to her heart, and she counts herself lucky to be able to be part of it with every shift at the bar, every bite of great food, and every last sip. This past year at Tales of the Cocktail 2016, Angel's "El Burro Catalan" won the Moscow Mule competition beating out hundreds of entries worldwide.

The Burgundian Muildier

CREATED BY BC Hoffman

Beverage Director, The Edison, Los Angeles, CA

INGREDIENTS

- 2 ounces Ketel One vodka
- ¾ ounce lemon juice
- Almond clove ginger cocoa rye soda, to top *(Pg. 189)*

DIRECTIONS

Shake vodka and lemon juice over ice, strain, and pour over fresh ice in a copper mug. Top with homemade almond clove ginger cocoa rye soda.

INSPIRATION

The inspiration for the recipe stems from the Burgundian feasts the Dutch used to have — which usually featured tons of meats studded with cloves and ginger, breads (mainly rye and pumpernickel), cheeses, and desserts with cocoa, almond, and pastries such as stroopwafel. I wanted to bring this historic meal to the classic mule, meshing Russian, Dutch and US creations to create a new classic.

BC *Hoffman*

 /bc.hoffman.5    @ChefBCfromDC

Chef BC Hoffman's love of food and entertaining began early on, in the kitchen of his Austrian grandmother, who was skilled in everything from doboshtorte to schnitzel. Born in Washington D.C., he quickly went from an apprenticeship in a sushi restaurant to working in Miami with James Beard Award winners Michelle Bernstein and Marvin Woods. A graduate of Johnson & Wales University, his must-have kitchen tools are the food processor and iron skillet, which he uses to cook up his favorite soul food comforts. In his free time, BC likes to spend time behind bars, and has honed his skills as a mixologist to create as many unique libations as there are days in the year. In addition to operating his own catering company, he is busy, teaching, training, mixing and cooking in Los Angeles. He has also had the opportunity to globally showcase his skills in numerous food and beverage competitions, and shows on Food Network, and via YouTube.

The Mafia Mule

CREATED BY *James Moreland*

Master Bar Expert, New York City, NY

INGREDIENTS

- 1 ½ ounces Punzoné organic vodka
- ½ ounce Amaro Montenegro
- Juice of ½ a small lime
- 4 ounce Q ginger beer
- Lemon peel, sprig of mint and fresh raspberries, for garnish

DIRECTIONS

Load up a copper mug with fresh ice, then add the vodka, the Amaro and the lime juice. Then top up the mug with ginger beer, add a nice chunk of lemon rind, a sprig of mint and a couple of fresh raspberries to garnish, then simply stir and serve.

INSPIRATION

One of the hidden gems in the culture of food and drink that still remains elusive is the aperitif cocktail. Amaros are some of the most complex aperitifs to both create and find in the world. In New York City, we are lucky to have great Italian food, wine and spirits — including the elusive Amaro, which here is lifted up by an equally inspired Italian spirit, Punzoné Organic Vodka.

James **Moreland**

 @JamesMoreland @moreland_neat

James Moreland is a first class mixologist whose inspired cocktails have graced the front pages of the *The New York Times* and *The Wall Street Journal* and is one of this generation's leading spirits authorities. With over 17 years in the industry, James Moreland enjoys a special relationship with the industry on both sides of the bar, his true passion. James Moreland's mastery at blending flavors and textures, creating a taste experience and enhancing the cocktail moment is beyond compare.

Photography by: Scott Weidman Photograp

The Karamazov

CREATED BY *Alex Haskell*

Owner and Beverage Program Director, Iron Station, Brooklyn, NY

INGREDIENTS

- 1 ½ ounces pink peppercorn infused vodka
- ½ ounce Barrow's Intense Ginger Liqueur
- ½ ounce cardamom syrup
- ½ ounce lime juice
- 2 dashes aromatic bitters
- Club soda
- Mint sprig, for garnish

DIRECTIONS

Combine pink peppercorn vodka, Barrow's Intense Ginger, cardamom syrup, bitters and lime juice in a shaker over ice. Shake until all the ingredients are well mixed. Bruise the mint sprig with your hand and place in copper mug with ice. Strain all ingredients from the mixer into your copper mug. Top with club soda and enjoy!

INSPIRATION

With the Karamazov, we wanted to create a more complex version of the traditional Moscow Mule. By infusing the vodka with pink peppercorns, we add a slight fruitiness and heat to the base. The cardamom syrup lends a subtle exotic sweetness to the cocktail. Barrow's Intense Ginger Liqueur is the purest expression of ginger we have ever tasted. We find some ginger beers to have residual chemical flavor notes, whereas the Barrow's brings only ginger to the party. The mint leaf serves as an aromatic, and helps to open your palate before the first sip.

Alex **Haskell**

 @ironstationbk

Alex Haskell is the rare native New Yorker. He was born and raised in Manhattan, and has been a proud Brooklyn resident for over 15 years. He has been in the hospitality industry since 2003, when he helped a friend open a small neighborhood bar in Carroll Gardens. There, Alex discovered his love of bartending, and subsequently that his degree in Economics from NYU was completely irrelevant. Since then, he has helped relaunch the Russian Tea Room, served as Wine Director for Lunetta, and spent several years honing his wine knowledge at Bar Veloce, before joining the opening team for Third & Vine in Jersey City as bar manager. He participated in the renowned Cocktails-in-the-Country program led by Gary Regan, and loves to create new infusions and juice combinations while pursuing unique and delicious cocktails. Alex loves dogs and wishes the Department of Health would let them hang out with him in his bar, Iron Station, which opened in Brooklyn in 2015.

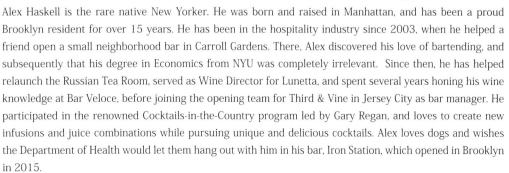

Mi Vida Mule

CREATED BY Spencer Taliaferro

Lead Mixologist, Lilt Lounge, Epic Hotel, Miami, FL

INGREDIENTS

- 1 ounce Hangar 1 Makrut Lime vodka
- 1 ounce Vida mezcal
- ¾ ounce lime juice
- ¾ ounce agave syrup
- 1 ounce passion fruit purée
- Pinch cayenne pepper
- Fever-Tree ginger beer, to top
- Sprig of mint, orange peel, for garnish

DIRECTIONS

Combine the vodka, mezcal, lime juice, agave syrup, passion fruit purée, and a pinch of cayenne pepper. Shake well, then fine strain over ice in a copper mug. Top with Fever-Tree ginger beer, and garnish with a nice bouquet of fresh mint and an expressed orange peel.

INSPIRATION

I really enjoy the smoky characteristics of mezcal, and the beautiful aromatics from the Makrut Lime vodka. I wanted to create a twist on the classic Moscow Mule, so I stuck with the fresh squeezed lime juice, and used agave syrup as my sugar component. The blend of the Makrut lime vodka, the mezcal, the passion fruit and the ginger beer is just a perfect match. At first you get spice from the ginger beer and the mezcal, subtle sweetness from the passion fruit, next you taste the cayenne pepper, and lastly the freshly squeezed lime juice brings everything together.

Spencer **Taliaferro**

f /legenddd ⊙ @spencenextlevel, @liltlounge

Currently the lead mixologist for the Lilt Lounge at Miami's Epic Hotel, Spencer has been bartending for 10 years. He was born and raised on a small island attached to Atlantic City, New Jersey. He moved to Miami four years ago, where he remains extremely passionate about creating interesting cocktails.

86

Photography by: Charity Faith Creative IG: @charityfa

Midtown Mule

CREATED BY *Rori Robinson*

Lead Bartender, The Spence, Atlanta, GA

INGREDIENTS

- 1 ½ ounces Absolut vodka
- 1 ounce house pineapple ginger syrup *(Pg. 186)*
- ½ ounce Dolin Blanc Vermouth
- ½ ounce lemon juice
- Club soda, to top

DIRECTIONS

In a shaker tin, combine all ingredients, except the club soda, and shake vigorously with ice. Strain over fresh ice into a copper mug, then top with club soda to fill. Garnish with a slice of fresh or candied ginger.

INSPIRATION

I wanted to create a mule that isn't overpowered by the flavor of ginger beer, which for me, can take over a drink's flavor profile completely. By using ginger in the syrup, the need for ginger beer is eliminated altogether, and the other natural citrus and herbal flavors are equally prominent in the drink.

Rori **Robinson**

f /rori.robinson   🐦 📷 @roritendsbar

Rori Robinson is an up-and-coming craft bartender in Atlanta, Georgia. She entered the hospitality arena as a fine dining server while attending Colorado State University. While she always had an interest in tending bar, she lacked the experience to land a position. Then, in 2013, opportunity struck when Rori asked her managers at The Spence in midtown Atlanta to cross-train her behind the bar instead of hiring a replacement for a bartender that was moving away. They agreed, and she remains on as their lead bartender and cocktail creator. With only three years behind the stick under her belt, Rori has begun to make a name for herself among industry insiders, with her specialty syrups and liqueurs, creative drink presentations, and passionate spirit.

Miso Mule

CREATED BY *Richard Woods AKA The Cocktail Guy*

Head of Cocktail & Spirit Development, Orange Brands Management, London, England

INGREDIENTS

- 1 ½ ounces Grey Goose vodka
- 1 ounce coconut miso sugar syrup **(Pg. 187)**
- ½ ounce lime juice
- ¼ ounce Coco López cream of coconut
- Old Jamaica ginger beer
- Dehydrated lime wheel and candied ginger, for garnish

DIRECTIONS

Shake all ingredients, except the ginger beer, with good quality cubed ice. Add ginger beer to the shaker and 'roll' to mix. Strain over fresh cubed ice into a copper mule mug. Garnish with a dehydrated lime wheel and a piece of candied ginger on a skewer.

INSPIRATION

I created this riff on a mule for one of our restaurant brands SUSHISAMBA —which features a unique blend of Japanese, Brazilian and Peruvian cuisine. Ultimately a drink should taste delicious, but I find that when using adventurous ingredients, classics are a good base for a cocktail, as it gives people something familiar to relate to. The twist in this drink is the miso, an integral part of the cuisine at SUSHISAMBA. Here it adds a lovely texture, as well as a sweet-savoury element.

Richard **Woods**

 @the_cocktailguy

Richard opened restaurants SUSHISAMBA and Duck and Waffle, both in London, in the summer of 2012. Since then, his role has developed into a global position, and he now oversees all of the Orange Brands restaurant group's locations from a creative and beverage standpoint. Prior to joining SUSHISAMBA, Richard was with Floridita, an iconic Cuban restaurant and bar from Havana. In his role as beverage director, he headed up the London location and oversaw new openings. Richard says it was the hospitality side of things that originally drew him to the bar and restaurant industry. Having now worked in several director positions, his creative mentality is that of an operator's mind with a bartender's heart.

Photography by: Evgeniy Vas

Blackcurrant Mule

CREATED BY *Alexey Proshkin*

Bartender, Ritz-Carlton, Moscow, Russia

INGREDIENTS

- 2 ounces coriander infused vodka *(Pg. 184)*
- 1 ounce blackcurrant purée *(Pg. 184)*
- ½ ounce ginger syrup
- ½ ounce lemon juice
- Soda water, to top
- Sprig of mint and freeze-dried blackcurrants, for garnish

DIRECTIONS

Pour all ingredients into a copper mug, add ice and gently stir with a bar spoon. Garnish with a sprig of mint and some freeze-dried blackcurrants.

INSPIRATION

When working on creating my own variation of the Moscow Mule, I decided that it should be prepared exclusively with ingredients local to Moscow. I love the blackcurrants in this drink — they can truly be called real Russian berries, and they pair very well with the ginger. The classic Moscow Mule recipe is quite simple: vodka, lime juice and ginger beer. I felt that any variation should include ginger, so I decided to use this wonderful pairing of the ginger and blackcurrant flavors. The lime I replaced with the more familiar Russian lemon. And of course, I added a generous helping of Russian vodka. It turned out tasty, but something was missing. I realized that in order to create a real Russian cocktail, it was not enough just to use local ingredients — it needed something more, a flavor that would convey a lot about my great country. Then it came to me — coriander. Every Russian person is familiar with the taste of rye black bread with coriander. This ingredient rounded out the flavor combination of the drink, making it a real Russian cocktail.

Alexey **Proshkin**

/proshkin.alexey @alexey_proshkin

Alexey Proshkin was born and raised in Moscow. He has worked as a bartender for more than 10 years, in over 15 of the finest bars and restaurants in Moscow, becoming one of the most well-known bartenders in Russia. Now, Alexey creates cocktails for the Ritz-Carlton Moscow, while also working various projects of his own. Throughout his entire career, Alexey has worked every day to improve his skills and knowledge, and to find the balance between efficiency and aesthetics.

The Elit Mule

CREATED BY *Jeffrey Morgenthaler*

Manager, Pepe Le Moko and Clyde Common, Portland, OR

INGREDIENTS

- 2 ounces Stoli Elit vodka
- 6 ounces of my house-made ginger beer *(Pg. 190)*
- 1/4 ounce fresh squeezed lime juice
- Lime, for garnish

DIRECTIONS

Place ice into a Moscow Copper Co. mug, and pour in the Stoli Elit vodka. Squeeze in fresh lime juice and top with my house-made ginger beer. Garnish with a lime wedge and enjoy.

INSPIRATION

My inspiration comes from a simple, fresh brewed ginger beer, as it should be made, with fresh ingredients.

Jeffrey **Morgenthaler**

   /jeffreymorgenthaler @jeffmorgen

Jeffrey Morgenthaler (Nightclub and Bar's Bartender of the Year, 2013), is an award-winning bartender (Tales of the Cocktail's American Bartender of the Year, 2016) and author of the first book devoted entirely to cocktail technique, *The Bar Book: Elements of Cocktail Technique* (Tales of the Cocktail's Best Spirits and Cocktail Writer, 2016). He currently manages the James Beard Award-nominated bar program at Clyde Common (Tales of the Cocktail's Best American Hotel Bar, 2014), and the celebrated Pepe Le Moko, both of which are located in Portland, Oregon.

Gin Mules

The world has the Dutch to thank for the existence of gin. "The Dutch invented it, the English refined it, and the Yanks glamorized it," according to the Esquire Drink Book, circa 1957. Gin's origins can be found in the Netherlands, where it developed from an early Dutch liquor known as jenever. Gin became popular in Great Britain when William of Orange, the leader of the Dutch Republic, occupied the English, Scottish and Irish thrones with his wife Mary. Essentially, gin is pure alcohol that has been flavored, primarily with juniper berries, but often with associated notes such as cassia bark, coriander seed, angelica root, anise seed, bitter orange peel, bitter almond, fennel, orris root, or a few ancillary herbs. As a result, gin has a distinctly botanical flavor, one that lends itself to more fragrant, herbaceous cocktails, such as the many recipes you'll find in this chapter.

Photography by: Bazil Zerins.

Bangkok Buckshot

CREATED BY *Konrad Cantor*

Part Owner, El Libre, New Orleans, LA

INGREDIENTS

- 2 ounces Aviation American Gin
- ½ ounces kaffir lime and lemongrass water *(Pg. 184)*
- ½ ounce galangal syrup *(Pg. 184)*
- ¼ teaspoon anhydrous citric acid
- Club soda, to top
- Sprig of cilantro, for garnish

DIRECTIONS

Combine all ingredients in an empty copper mug. Fill with four cubes of Kold-Draft ice, and top with club soda. Stir. Garnish with a generous sprig of cilantro.

INSPIRATION

While many of my cocktails are Cuban, for this mule I took my inspiration from Thailand. The drink features galangal, which is a wonderful substitution for those who love a ginger syrup — and it packs more of a punch. The drink is vegan friendly, and the ingredients stay true to most traditional Thai dishes, including the sprig of cilantro as a garnish.

Konrad **Cantor**

f /konrad.kantor.94   @ellibrenola

Konrad Cantor currently makes drinks, coffee and even food at El Libre, a quaint French Quarter charmer where he is part owner. El Libre is inspired by Cuban/South Floridian street food, Cuban coffee a la Cafe Bustelo, and features a short but highly optimized menu of classic Cuban cocktails. El Libre, measuring at a mere four-feet-three-and-one-half inches, is the smallest craft cocktail bar in the city of New Orleans.

Blossoms on Silk Road

CREATED BY *Jake Bliven*

Bar Development at Ounce, Bittersweet & Something Beautiful, Taipei, Taiwan

INGREDIENTS

- 1 ½ ounces Aviation American Gin
- ½ ounce Dolin Génépy des Alpes
- ¾ ounce fresh lime juice
- ¾ ounce chai ginger syrup *(Pg. 184)*
- 2 dashes Bittercube Corazón bitters
- 2 ounces East Imperial Yuzu Tonic
- 3-4 basil leaves
- Lime wheel, for garnish

DIRECTIONS

Add bitters, lime juice, chai ginger syrup and basil leaves to a mixing tin and give it a light muddle. Next add Aviation and Génépy, as well as cracked ice and shake for eight seconds. Double strain into an ice filled copper mug, and top with yuzu tonic water. Stir to incorporate and add straw. Garnish with a lime wheel stuffed with a tuft of basil through the center, floated on top of the drink. Serve with a smile.

INSPIRATION

I wanted to take an American distillate and showcase it with a Far Eastern culinary influence. I love utilizing Aviation gin, as it's a wonderful spirit and they have some of the best individuals in the industry working for them. The name refers to a donkey featured in older American TV shows and the silk road is considered one of the most influential and historical spice trade routes in history, one that connected Eastern civilization with Western civilization The name just seemed ideal after the creation of the cocktail recipe.

Jake **Bliven**

f /jake.bliven.16   @SD_JakeyB

Jake Bliven has been working in the beverage industry for over 18 years, in the Northwest and in California. After several years of bar management, he now focuses on consulting for upcoming projects, and has also been known to assist in the development of distribution companies, craft breweries and micro distilleries. Working with wonderful people is the one element that binds all these facets of the industry, and the reason he loves working in the hospitality field. Jake won second place at the 2016 Tales of the Cocktail competition, which included hundreds of entries from all over the world.

Buck the French

CREATED BY *Ron Oleksa*

The Cellar at Duckworth's, Charlotte, NC

INGREDIENTS

- 3 ounces Prosecco
- 1 ounce Bluecoat gin
- 1 ½ teaspoons fresh ground ginger
- ½ ounce lemon juice
- ½ ounce simple syrup
- ½ ounce Lillet Blanc
- 2 dashes Angostura bitters

DIRECTIONS

Place all ingredients — except for Prosecco and bitters — in a large shaker. Add ice. Shake hard for 15-20 seconds. Double strain into mule mug. Top with Prosecco and the two dashes of Angostura bitters.

INSPIRATION

This drink was based on the classic French '75 Champagne cocktail.

Ron **Oleksa**

@cocktailcraftsmannc

With over 20 years of experience behind the stick in Charlotte, Ron Oleksa has experienced the evolution of the bar scene. From putting together award-winning cocktail lists at eclectic lounges, to selecting and managing over 40 wines by the glass at charming local neighborhood restaurants, or offering the best of local craft beers at a Carolina BBQ biker bar, it has always been his goal to offer a quality array of varied flavors. Ron's passion for precisely using quality ingredients to develop layers of complexity is apparent with the first sip of one of his handcrafted cocktails. He is looking forward to helping further the progression of the Charlotte palate by offering the very best libations, using new and classic techniques, and always continuing to improve and evolve. Ron currently runs the bar program at The Cellar at Duckworth's in the heart of downtown Charlotte. Offering the widest selection of Amari and the best barrel-aging program in town, this venue concentrates on using fresh ingredients and smaller brand craft liquors.

Just Beet It

CREATED BY *Andrew Larson*

Creative Lead, The Nolen, San Diego, CA

INGREDIENTS

- 1 ½ ounces Aviation American Gin
- ½ ounce fresh juiced beets
- ½ ounce fresh ginger syrup *(equal parts juiced ginger root and sugar)*
- ½ ounce fresh lemon juice
- ½ ounce cinnamon syrup *(8 cinnamon sticks boiled with one-to-one parts simple syrup and water)*
- 1 egg white
- Soda water

DIRECTIONS

Combine all ingredients into a shaking tin, omitting the soda water. Dry shake for 10 seconds. Add ice. Shake again vigorously for 20 seconds. Add soda water to the bottom of the mug. Fine strain the cocktail mixture into the mule mug. Top with additional soda if desired. Add a few drops of bitters, as desired, and garnish with a sprig of fresh mint.

INSPIRATION

Ginger-beet juice is a favorite beverage of my significant other, she drinks it almost every morning. One day I had the idea of making a bartender approved version. A bit of protein, fresh juice, some spice from the ginger and cinnamon and you can't forget the gin!

Andrew **Larson**

 @simplystirred

Andrew Larson was born into the hospitality industry, and was taught by some of the industry's finest in the Pacific North West. He has worked in both the front and back of house, where his love of food has helped to shape his love of cocktails. After a five-year stint in Seattle working at RN74 and Tavern Law — and consequently learning from some incredibly talented people — Andrew moved to San Diego in February 2016 to become the Creative Lead at The Nolen. His goal is to take craft cocktails and make them approachable to everyone. He loves to share his spirit knowledge with his guests and is always ready to make fun, unique creations.

Royal Tart

CREATED BY *Andreea Jula*

Bartender, Bovine & Barley, Houston, TX

INGREDIENTS

- 3 fresh raspberries
- 1 small slice of fresh ginger (nickel sized), peeled
- 2 ounces Earl Grey infused Aviation American Gin
  (1 teabag per 2 cups gin for 2 hours)
- 1 ounce simple syrup
- ¾ ounce fresh lemon juice
- 5 drops 18.21 Ginger Lemon tincture
- 3 dashes Fee Brothers Rhubarb bitters
- 2 dashes Fee Brothers Black Walnut bitters
- Sparkling water

DIRECTIONS

In a shaking tin, muddle fresh ginger slice and raspberries. Add the infused gin, the fresh lemon juice, the syrup, the ginger lemon tincture, the rhubarb and walnut bitters. Add ice about 3/4 of the way in the small tin. Shake vigorously. Double strain through a Hawthorne and mesh cone strainer over ice into a copper mug. Top with sparkling water (I used Topo Chico). Garnish with a slice of lemon and a fresh raspberry.

INSPIRATION

I wanted a cocktail that would reflect my bubbly personality, so my inspiration was Princess Bubblegum from the *Adventure Time* series. She has a tart recipe with strawberries, so I went to the market and let the colorful fruit and vegetable stands guide me through pairing things that play with the taste buds. Rhubarb, although it looks like a vegetable, is actually a fruit. Its tart, bubble gum flavor made me think of combining it with raspberries, but wanted a bit of a kick, which is why I added the walnut bitters and the Earl Grey-infused gin.

Andreea **Jula**

f /andreea.jula88 .@cereal4days

Bartending is a relatively new craft for Andreea Jula, having been behind the bar for just under a year now. Her path to bartending began by working next to people who were very advanced cocktail enthusiasts. She joined USBG when she first started out, and began attending cocktail conferences, seminars and events that further immersed her and helped her fall in love with the craft. Always having been interested in homeopathy and living a healthy lifestyle, Andreea works with herbs, spices and many all-natural ingredients in her cocktails.

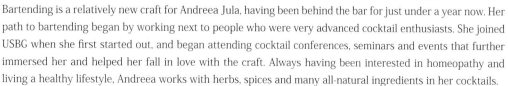

The Cutler Family Tradition

CREATED BY *Ian Cutler*

Owner and Head Distiller, Cutler's Artisan Spirits, Santa Barbara, CA

INGREDIENTS

- 2 ounces Cutler's gin
- ¾ ounce heavy cream
- 1 small egg white (optional but recommended)
- ¾ ounce simple syrup
- 1/8 teaspoon orange flower water
- 1 teaspoon ginger puree
- ½ ounce fresh squeezed lime juice
- ¼ ounce fresh squeezed lemon juice
- 2 ¾ ounces strong flavored ginger beer

DIRECTIONS

Combine gin, heavy cream, egg white, orange flower water, simple syrup, and ginger puree in a cocktail shaker. Shake vigorously for 30 seconds. Add ice, lemon and lime juices and shake for at least another 30 seconds. Pour gently into a copper mule mug, being careful not to pour out any frothy head. Add ginger beer to the mug and stir gently. Top with any frothy head left in the shaker and garnish with lemon and lime slices.

INSPIRATION

The Cutler Family Tradition combines one of the Cutler family's favorite cocktails, the great Ramos Gin Fizz, with a traditional Gin Buck. Combining these two cocktails creates a creamy floral spin on a gin-based Moscow Mule cocktail. This combination of classic cocktails is a perfect fit for the Original Moscow Copper Co. mug.

Ian **Cutler**

@sb_distilling

Ian Cutler is owner and head distiller for Cutler's Artisan Spirits located in Santa Barbara, California. Cutler's is the first distillery in Santa Barbara, and continues a long family heritage in California liquor, dating back four generations to Ian's great grandfather, Duke Cutler, a renowned moonshiner and bootlegger from California's gold country.

Seven Sons Mule

CREATED BY *Ozborne Williams*

Bartender, Broadway Bar, Los Angeles, CA

INGREDIENTS

- 2 ounces Hendrick's gin
- ½-¾ ounces fresh lime juice
- 2 slices fresh cucumber
- Fever-Tree ginger beer, to top
- Lime twist, luxardo black cherries and mint, for garnish

DIRECTIONS

Muddle two slices of cucumber in a mixing glass. Add gin and lime and shake over a few ice cubes, for no more than three to five seconds. Strain contents of the mixing glass over a copper mug filled with ice, top off with Fever-Tree ginger beer, and add garnish.

INSPIRATION

I love Hendrick's martinis, and thought it would make a delicious mule-style cocktail. This take is a little different than the classic Moscow Mule with vodka, but it retains the essence of the traditional mule. Hendrick's gin is such a delicate, fresh, and subtle spirit with its infusion of cucumber, which mixed with the fresh lime, muddled cucumber and ginger beer gives you the perfect balance of freshness with a little zest! The name Seven Sons Mule pays homage to William Grant (the founder of the company that now makes Hendrick's gin) and his seven sons that helped him build the distillery back in 1886 in Scotland.

Ozborne **Williams**

 /ozborne.williams @TheBigOzee @thebigoz

Ozborne Williams began bartending in Seattle in 1993 with no experience, landing his first bartending gig on the basis of his personality alone. When he headed back east in 1995 to attend college, he got a gig at a local pub in Greenwich, Connecticut. It was a job that not only helped put him through college, but taught him about working in a fast paced bar, and allowed him to learn firsthand what being a "rock star bartender" was all about. After heading home to Seattle in 2003, Ozborne then moved to Los Angeles in 2004, and in the spring of 2005 he took a job at Downtown LA's Broadway Bar, telling himself "This is the last place I'll ever bartend." Eleven years later, he's still there. Ozborne considers himself an old school bartender, and loves everything that bartending entails. He feels that bartenders are the caretakers of the hospitality industry, in that they create delicious cocktails to help celebrate the victories and ease the hardships of life, and always provide memorable experiences for anyone who walks up to their bar.

Queen of Cups

CREATED BY *Matthew Murphy*

Lead Bartender, The Elephant, Baltimore, MD

INGREDIENTS

- 1 ounce Pimm's No 1
- ¾ ounce Amaro Montenegro
- ½ ounce Aviation American Gin
- ½ ounce lemon juice
- 2 slices cucumber
- Fever-Tree ginger beer

DIRECTIONS

Muddle cucumber in a shaker tin, and add all ingredients, except the ginger beer. Give it a short shake, then strain into a copper mug, over ice. Top off with ginger beer, to fill the mug, and garnish with a cucumber ribbon.

INSPIRATION

The classic Pimm's Cup was my inspiration for this cocktail. The addition of cucumber makes it really cool and refreshing, particularly on a balmy Baltimore afternoon.

Matthew **Murphy**

@mattpmurph

Matthew Murphy has been bartending since 2001. In that time he has held jobs in everything from neighborhood bars and Irish Pubs, to upscale hotels and restaurants. He is currently serving up globally-inspired drinks and cuisine as the bar manager at The Elephant in Baltimore, Maryland.

Pedal Tone

CREATED BY *Marisa Miller*

Bartender, Local Edition, San Francisco, CA

INGREDIENTS

- 1 ½ ounces hibiscus-infused Aviation American Gin
  (Pg. 188)
- 1 ounce lime juice
- ¾ ounce Giffard Ginger of the Indies
- ½ ounce Raft Hibiscus Lavender syrup
- ½ ounce Top Note Indian tonic concentrate
- 2 dashes The Bitter Housewife lime coriander bitters
- ¾ ounce soda water
- Lime wheel, approx. ¼ inch thick, for garnish

DIRECTIONS

Add all ingredients, minus the soda water, to a copper mug. Fill the mug about three-quarters of the way full with crushed ice. Stir briefly to incorporate the ingredients. Add soda, then top off with more crushed ice. Garnish the rim of the mug with a lime wheel.

INSPIRATION

The trumpet-shaped flowers of the hibiscus lend themselves well to the vibrant and energetic jazz music that is quintessentially New Orleans. To pay homage to the rhythms that move the unique city, I named my cocktail Pedal Tone, the fundamental note in a harmonic series.

Marisa **Miller**

 /marisamm    @marcarism

Marisa started bartending as a way to put herself through college. By the time she had finished her degree in Chemistry, she had already found her calling. Fifteen years later, she is still bartending, very happily working behind the stick at San Francisco's Local Edition. Her analytical background provides a unique approach for blending flavor profiles while creating cocktails.

Lordship Mule

CREATED BY *Jarrod Cuffe*

Founder, Off the Cuffe Bitter Solutions, Dublin, Ireland

INGREDIENTS

- 1 ounce Pusser's Rum Original Admiralty Blend
- ½ ounce Aviation American Gin
- 1/3 ounce blended rhubarb and ginger jam
- ½ ounce fresh lime juice
- 4 dashes habanero chili tincture
- Gosling's ginger beer, to fill
- Sprig of mint, for garnish

DIRECTIONS

Build the drink in a copper mug, over cubed ice, adding the ginger beer last. Garnish with a large sprig of mint.

INSPIRATION

I was originally inspired whilst working on Lordship Lane in London, an old haunt of retired admiralty, where only drinks made with rum and gin would do. I felt it needed a bit more of a kick to get these old mules moving, and the addition of rhubarb and habanero chili does the trick.

Jarrod **Cuffe**

 @jecuffe @offthecuffe_bitters

Jarrod Cuffe, who was once a chef, has always believed in the importance of flavor balance. A desire to focus more on customer interaction brought him to the front of house, where he found his hands in the ice. Originally from Australia, Jarrod has moved all over Europe working in bars in Paris, London and Dublin. Since landing in Dublin, Jarrod founded Off the Cuffe Bitter Solutions, to create artisanal bitters locally in the city of Dublin.

Mezcal & Tequila Mules

While all too often associated with shots or margaritas, tequila is a sophisticated liquor that today comes in many different varieties. This popular Mexican spirit is distilled from the blue agave plant, primarily in the area surrounding the city of Tequila, 40 miles northwest of Guadalajara, and in the highlands of the central western Mexican state of Jalisco. The flavor of tequila can vary greatly according to the region in which the blue agave was grown. Plants grown in the highlands often yield sweeter and fruitier-tasting tequila, while lowland agaves are known to produce tequila with an earthier flavor. Resting and aging techniques can also influence the color and flavor of tequila. Another spirit that hails from Mexico, and has become increasingly popular in recent years, is mezcal. Unlike tequila, which is made only from the blue agave plant, mezcal can be made from over 30 different varietals of the agave species. Mezcal is always made from the heart of the agave plant, known as the "piña". Once removed from the agave plants, the piñas are roasted underground in pit ovens for around several days, a process which gives mezcal its intense and distinctly smoky flavor. The piñas are then turned into a mash, which is fermented and distilled, and sometimes aged in wooden barrels, depending on the type of mezcal being produced. While traditionally enjoyed straight, its distinctive smoky flavor makes mezcal a potent addition to cocktails, such as many of the recipes on the following pages.

Mezcal Mule

CREATED BY *Jim Meehan*

Bartender, Journalist and Proprietor of Mixography Inc., Portland, OR

INGREDIENTS

- 1 ½ ounces Sombra mezcal
- 1 ounce house ginger beer
- ¾ ounce lime juice
- ¾ ounce Boiron passion fruit purée
- ½ ounce agave syrup
- 4 cucumber slices (reserve one for garnish)
- Candied ginger and a pinch ground chili, for garnish

DIRECTIONS

Muddle the agave syrup and cucumber, then add remaining ingredients. Shake with ice, then fine strain into a chilled copper mug filled with ice. Garnish with a piece of candied ginger picked to a slice of cucumber, then add a pinch of ground chili on top.

INSPIRATION

I developed this cocktail for Richard Betts in the winter of 2009, as a signature cocktail for his new mezcal brand Sombra, and have served it at PDT ever since. The idea was to accentuate the earthy, vegetal qualities of the mezcal with the ginger root and cucumber, and brighten the mixture with tropical passionfruit. Spice and heat are common in Mexican cuisine, so I garnish the drink with a pinch of chili.

Jim **Meehan**

  @mixography

Jim Meehan's career in the bar business spans over 20 years, including stints in Madison, Wisconsin and New York City. Besides tending and running bars — including his James Beard Award winning Portland establishment PDT — Jim is the author of *The PDT Cocktail Book*, a contributor to *Lucky Peach* magazine, and the national mixologist for American Express's Centurion Lounges. He currently resides in Portland, Oregon, where he oversees his consulting firm Mixography Inc.

Oaxaca Muletail

CREATED BY *Stella Snyder*

Bartender, Cardinal Spirits, Bloomington, IN

INGREDIENTS

- 1 ½ ounces Montelobos mezcal
- ¾ ounce fresh lime juice
- ½ ounce Liber & Co. pineapple gum syrup
- 2-3 dashes The Bitter Housewife lime coriander bitters
- Top with East Imperial Thai dry ginger ale

DIRECTIONS

Blend mezcal, lime, and pineapple gum syrup in a copper mule mug. Top with ginger ale and bitters, and then stir briefly to mix ingredients. Garnish with a three pineapple leaf fan.

INSPIRATION

My sister's amazing fruit salad, which contains pineapple, among other fruits, plus cilantro and ginger.

Stella **Synder**

 /stella.snyder.14   @stellarenee12

Stella Snyder has bartended for 12 years in the Midwest, recently for the esteemed Wellmann's Brands in Cincinnati, Ohio, and now for Cardinal Spirits, the craft distillery in Bloomington, Indiana. Aside from bartending, she holds a Master's degree in biology and she teaches yoga therapy to cancer patients in Indianapolis hospitals. Mixing craft cocktails has become one of her passions, and Stella enjoys applying Ayurvedic seasonal food guidelines to her cocktails' ingredients, to help create balance. She loves bourbon and mezcal, and any cocktail with an interesting story behind it.

Photography by: Erwin Ce

Aztec Mule

CREATED BY *Rakshit Khurana*

Beverage Training Manager, MMI Bar Academy, Dubai, United Arab Emirates

INGREDIENTS

- 2 ounces Montelobos mezcal
- 1 ounce blueberry-ginger shrub *(Pg. 184)*
- 3 ounces Fever-Tree ginger beer

DIRECTIONS

Pour ingredients in a copper mug, over ice. Garnish with a wedge of lime.

INSPIRATION

The Aztec Mule was inspired by the long-standing traditional American drink, the Switchel, which originated in the Caribbean in the 17th century, and served as a cooling drink in the sweltering heat. A Switchel is traditionally made with ginger, sweetener, apple cider vinegar and lengthened with water. I needed something potent in taste to match the power of ginger in the mule, so I chose mezcal. The choice of spirit was also inspired by the rising popularity of mezcal, which is why I called it the Aztec Mule. Finally, I chose to use Fever-Tree ginger beer, because of its all natural ingredients, and because one of the locations where they source their ginger is Kochi, in India, which is my home country and has a special place in my heart.

Rakshit **Khurana**

f /rakshit.khurana.71   @baracademyatmmi

Rakshit is the Beverage Training Manager at the MMI Bar Academy in Dubai. He began his career working as a barback in his home country of India, and has been associated with the world of hospitality ever since. His work has given him the opportunity to travel to all seven continents, and make friends across the world over the past 12 years. He has been educating and training hospitality personnel for over four years now, and has represented most of the major league liquor companies during this time, previously in India and now in the United Arab Emirates and Africa.

Mezican Mule

CREATED BY Renick "JR" Lambey

Mixology Consultant (Sirmixologist) and Cocktail Batch Mix (Beyond Batched, Inc.), Los Angeles, CA

INGREDIENTS

- 2 ounces mezcal
- ¾ ounce lemon and lime juice mix
- ¼ ounce cucumber
- ¼ ounce kiwi fruit
- 1 sprig of sage
- 1 slice jalapeño
- 1 piece candied ginger, for garnish
- Freshly cracked black pepper, for garnish
- Ginger syrup soda

DIRECTIONS

Muddle the sage, jalapeño, kiwi and cucumber in a shaker with lemon and lime juice. Pour in mezcal and ice. Shake well with ice in the shaker tin, then strain over ice into the mule mug. Pour ginger syrup soda on top, and garnish with skewered ginger and sage. Flake freshly cracked black pepper on top, and singe the sage with a match.

INSPIRATION

This spin on the Moscow Mule is catered to new enthusiasts of mezcal and traditionalists who love a bold scotch cocktail. If you can imagine a Penicillin (a cocktail that blends scotch, honey ginger syrup and fresh lemon juice) with personality and a lava pit for a playground. This tropical concoction offers up a little taste of Mexico's pride, California's love and Hawaii's freedom.

Renick **"JR" Lambey**

 @sirmixologist

Sirmixologist originally hails from Los Angeles, but his interest in mixology began while he was studying undergrad at the University of Colorado at Boulder. He then moved to New York City, and began working in the trading side of the finance business. After two years in New York, he started playing around with mixology at home. Three years into "just playing around at home" he joined a cocktail catering group and began constructing programs for events. Soon, he ended up working with world renowned chef Jean-Georges Vongerichten at The Mercer Kitchen. From there, he began working with top chefs such as Roy Choi and Jeremy Spector on collaborations. He also began developing his own brand, and marketing a new way to deliver fresh and organic classic and craft cocktails. Since then, he has been consulting in bar and restaurant development, cocktail programs, hosting cocktail events and distributing his own batched mix juices for cocktails.

Diablo Mango Mule

CREATED BY *Kimber Weissert*

Head Bartender, Wallace's Taproom, Pittsburgh, PA

INGREDIENTS

- 1 ½ ounces Montelobos mezcal
- 1 ounce Ancho Reyes chili liqueur
- 1 ounce Perfect Purée mango purée
- 1 ounce fresh lime juice
- 5 dashes Hella Bitters Smoked Chili bitters
- Barritt's ginger beer, to top
- Dried chili mango piece, and lime peels, for garnish

DIRECTIONS

In a shaker, combine mezcal, Ancho Reyes, mango purée, lime juice and bitters. Add ice and shake. Strain into a copper mule mug, add fresh ice, and top with ginger beer. Garnish with a piece of dried chili mango, rolled into a rose, with two small lime peels, on a cocktail pin.

INSPIRATION

My favorite Mexican treat, dried chili mango pieces. When I was a child, a family friend would bring dried chili mango back after traveling to Mexico, and to me it was always a very special treat. So I thought, why not make a favorite childhood treat into a fantastic cocktail?!

Kimber **Weissert**

f /Kimber.weissert 🐦 @kimbosliced86 📷 @kimberlw

Kimber Weissert is a Pittsburgh bartender who has been working the craft for about eight years. She began her bartending journey at Peabody's Down Under, a concert venue in Cleveland, where she was also a talent buyer by day. She served beer, shots, and basic drinks back in those days. As the years went on, her interest in classic and craft cocktails blossomed. Kimber read both classic and modern cocktail books to absorb everything she could, and she soon began to experiment. In 2013, Kimber moved back to her hometown of Pittsburgh and really began to focus on learning the craft. She joined the USBG in Pittsburgh to get more involved with the cocktail community, and to learn everything she could from her peers. Her hard work paid off this past year when she won regionals in Pittsburgh for the 2016 Woodford Reserve Manhattan Experience, and was one of six finalists picked to compete in the finals held in New York City. Kimber says what she enjoys most about bartending is the creative process — and surprising her clientele with new tastes of unique cocktails and twists on the classics. Although a bourbon girl at heart, she says that in reality she loves all spirits. After all, who can turn down a good Aviation, a Moscow Mule or a great Manhattan?

Wise Oaxacan Mule

CREATED BY *Jennifer Schommer*

Recipe Designer, Common Man Cocktails, Hudson, NH

INGREDIENTS

- 10 pieces of ginger
- 10 sage leaves
- 1 ½ ounces Elijah Craig small batch bourbon
- 1 ounce Montelobos mezcal
- ¾ ounce honey
- ¾ ounce fresh lemon juice
- 2 ounces Q ginger beer

DIRECTIONS

Muddle sage and ginger with honey and lemon juice in a shaker. Add ice and remaining ingredients, except ginger beer. Shake for about 30 seconds or until chilled. Double strain into a copper mug filled with crushed ice. Garnish with a sage sprig.

INSPIRATION

My inspiration for The Wise Oaxacan Mule, my retake on the Moscow Mule, was my maturing cocktail tastes. A year or two ago, I would have created a much different drink, most likely containing rum. Don't get me wrong – I love rum. But I have branched out and tried other alcohols and flavors. I wanted to complement the ginger flavor found in the original Moscow Mule. What better way to complement a flavor than with the dynamic taste of herbs? I tried a few different herbs and determined that sage worked the best. I am quite proud of the flavors found in the drink and also amazed that I created a drink using bourbon and mezcal.

Jennifer **Schommer**

Jennifer Schommer produces cocktail episodes with occasional guest appearances on the popular YouTube channel Common Man Cocktails. She began creating cocktail recipe designs for sponsored brands on the channel, as well as custom recipe designs for fans of the show. She has used the eight years experience tasting and designing cocktails behind the scenes on the YouTube channel to help advance her own cocktail creations. Recently, she has launched her own cocktail e-book series on homecocktailmenu.com, for customers hosting events and parties.

Hakka Mule

CREATED BY *Brian Callahan*

Bartender, Tiger Mama, Boston, MA

INGREDIENTS

- 1 ounce Montelobos mezcal
- ¾ ounce Appleton Estate Signature Blend rum
- ½ ounce Giffard Banane du Bresil liqueur
- ¼ ounce Giffard Orgeat syrup
- ¾ ounce fresh lime juice
- 15 drops Bittercube Jamaican No. 2 bitters
- 2 ounces Chinese 5 Spice Ginger Beer *(Pg. 186)*

DIRECTIONS

Combine all ingredients except ginger beer, and shake over ice. Add two ounces Chinese five spice ginger beer, and strain into mule mug over Kold-Draft cubes. Garnish with a sprig of mint.

INSPIRATION

For the Hakka Mule, I wanted to combine Chinese five spice, a key ingredient in many Asian cuisines, with some of the staples that make up tiki cocktail culture. While they hail from two completely different cultures, ingredients such as cinnamon, ginger, star anise, and banana are flavors that work so well together in both Asian and Caribbean cuisine. Then I turned to my personal favorite Moscow Mule variation, the Oaxaca Mule, and added the mezcal for some back-bone. The name Hakka refers to a Chinese subgroup made up primarily of laborers, that originat-edin Northern China. In Chinese, "Hakka" translates directly to "guest family" which refers to the several migrations the Hakka people have been forced to make due to social unrest, upheaval, and invasions. In the mid-19th to early 20th century, there was a massive migration of Hakka people to Jamaica. To this day, Jamaica is home to one of the largest Hakka populations outside of China.

Brian **Callahan**

 @bcal889

Originally hailing from Stamford, Connecticut, Brian Callahan moved to Boston in the Summer of 2014 to pursue a career in the music industry. After taking a job waiting tables to help pay the bills, he was soon offered an opportunity to barback, and eventually bartend at Grafton Street in Harvard Square. Soon realizing where his true passions lie, he left the music business behind and hasn't looked back since. Today you can find him behind the bar at Tiger Mama, just down the road from Boston's historic Fenway Park, where he is known for his witty jokes, and powerful, dashingly handsome eyebrows.

Pacific Moon

CREATED BY *Adam Stearns*

Resort Mixologist, Terranea, Rancho Palos Verdes, CA

INGREDIENTS

- 1 ½ ounces Herradura Reposado tequila
- ¾ ounce Noilly Prat Ambre vermouth
- 1 ounce pomegranate hibiscus shrub **(Pg. 188)**
- Fever-Tree ginger beer
- A spritz of La Nina Primario mezcal
- Candied ginger and apple fan, for garnish

DIRECTIONS

Add all ingredients but the ginger beer and mezcal into a shaker, then strain over crushed ice into a copper mug. Top with Fever Tree ginger beer and spritz or lace La Nina Primario mezcal over the top. Garnish with an apple fan and candied ginger, and serve.

INSPIRATION

This cocktail was primarily inspired by seasonality, but also from the focus of our restaurant Mar'sel. At this restaurant, we are kitchen driven with an incredible wine list — so all of our cocktails feature wine in some way, shape or form. I have been learning from the kitchen more and more, and have been inspired to incorporate ingredients that I need to turn a stove on to prepare. So, I make the shrub and the candied ginger myself, and strive to improve the flavors and balance each time I use these techniques.

Adam **Stearns**

 @chril18

Adam wears the job title of Resort Mixologist at Terranea Resort in Rancho Palos Verdes, California. He can be found behind the bar at Mar'sel, the resort's signature restaurant. He is responsible for working VIP functions, as well as cultivating menus and working with the teams behind each of the property's 10 bars. Adam has been in the industry for 15 years, and been bartending for the last decade. He moved to California around five years ago after a stint in Connecticut, and is inspired by the constantly evolving bar community and culture on the West Coast.

Tequila Hot Mule

CREATED BY *Daniel Fast*

Founder of BARchitecture, Las Vegas, NV

INGREDIENTS

- 1 ½ ounces Don Julio Blanco tequila
- ½ ounce Monin habanero lime syrup
- ½ ounce fresh lime juice
- 2 pieces dried Chile de árbol, one for muddling, one for garnish
- Gosling's ginger beer
- Cinnamon stick, for garnish

DIRECTIONS

Muddle one piece of dried Chile de árbol in shaker tin. Add the rest of ingredients, except the ginger beer. Double strain over fresh ice, then top with Gosling's ginger beer. Garnish with remaining piece of dried Chile de Arbol, and a dusting of cinnamon stick.

INSPIRATION

This cocktail's inspiration came from a desire to take the road less traveled. I like to challenge my skill set and always push myself to try new things — I prefer innovation to repetition. The spicy notes of the chile, ginger and cinnamon blend perfectly for a well-balanced cocktail.

Daniel **Fast**

Daniel Fast has been working in the hospitality industry for nearly two decades, the latter half spent in Las Vegas. He is the founder of BARchitecture, a bar and nightlife consulting group. His drinks have been featured on a variety of menus both on and off the Las Vegas strip, including Hyde nightclub at the Bellagio. His concept of what he likes to call "functional mixology" has proven very successful — crafting complex flavors with approachable techniques.

BARchitecture.CO

Zinger Meets Mezcal

CREATED BY *Daniel Maldonado*

Craft Bartender, Tanner's, Huntington Beach, CA

INGREDIENTS

- 1 ½ ounces Montelobos mezcal
- ½ ounces Ancho Reyes chili liqueur
- ½ ounce fresh squeezed lime juice
- ¼ ounce simple syrup
- Top off with homemade hibiscus ginger soda

(Pg. 191)

DIRECTIONS

Pour the mezcal, Ancho Reyes, lime juice and simple syrup in a shaker and shake. Strain the mixture over clean ice into a copper mug. Top off the drink with homemade hibiscus ginger soda. Garnish with a lime wheel, hibiscus, dried ginger and a sprig of mint.

INSPIRATION

Growing up in Mexico is the best gift I have ever had — it is so rich in culture. You can eat so many different varieties of food and spend all day staring at the beautiful landscapes. My mission is to capture a tiny part of that essence of Mexico in a cocktail.

Daniel **Maldonado**

 f /daniel.alejandro.maldonado @dany.maldonado0

Daniel Maldonado began studying the culinary arts in Mexico when he was 18 years of age. Early on in his studies, some time mid-term, he discovered the bartending world by accident. One day, his university class went to a mall to install an information booth to recruit new students, and the booth was offering complimentary non-alcoholic drinks. That's the first time Daniel had heard about and mixed a "mocktail." Five years later, he can be found behind the bar Tanner's, a bar and restaurant in Huntington Beach, California, where he is honing his cocktail craft and mastering the art of mixology.

Oaxacan Mule

—✦—

CREATED BY *Rob Mariani*

Bartender, Alley Twenty Six, Durham, NC

INGREDIENTS

- 1 ½ ounces Montelobos mezcal
- ½ ounce Ancho Reyes chile liqueur
- 1 ounce housemade ginger syrup *(Pg. 187)*
- ½ ounce fresh lime juice
- Splash of soda water

DIRECTIONS

Add crushed ice to copper mug. Add a splash of soda. Then add the ginger syrup, lime juice and liquors. Swizzle. Garnish with candied ginger and lime twist. Hang candied ginger in rim. Drape twist across top of drink with one end on the ginger.

INSPIRATION

"Cold war kid to southern bartender." I was born in Tallinn, Estonia. I now live in Durham, North Carolina. Like many people from cold places, I gravitate toward warm places. While living in Los Angeles, I came to love Mexican cuisine – and, of course – agave spirits. Thus, I took this LA-born drink a bit further south. The spice from the ginger and the smoke from the mezcal pair perfectly with the smoky spice from the Ancho Reyes. Watch out — this Mule can kick!

Robert *Mariani*

f robert.mariani.18 🅞 @behindthestickprovisions, @robmariani42

Born in Estonia and raised in NYC, Robert Mariani started his bartending career in 2003 while traveling through New Zealand. After honing his cocktail skills in high-end restaurants in Washington D. C., he relocated to North Carolina. Robert has been working at the cocktail bar Alley Twenty Six in Durham and in 2015, he and owner Shannon Healy started the company Behind the Stick Provisions, LLC, making and selling handcrafted tonic syrups and other cocktail ingredients.

Whiskey Mules

Scotch, Whiskey, Bourbon & Rye

Whiskies are beautiful, rich, caramel-hued spirits that generally have long histories and complex flavor profiles. But many people get confused about the differences between Scottish whisky, Irish whiskey and American whiskies, also known as bourbon and rye. So, let's break it down. Whisky or whiskey is a broad term that generally categorizes distilled alcoholic beverages made from fermented grain mash (those grains being barley, corn, rye or wheat). The main difference between Scotch, whiskey and bourbon is geographic, but also involves different ingredients and spellings. If your drink of choice is labeled Scotch, it must have been 100% made in Scotland, using malted barley, and aged in oak casks for no less than three years. The Irish also make their whiskey using malted barley, and age it for at least three years in wooden casks. They simply spell it with the -ey, due to the Irish translation of the classical Gaelic word for water, from which the term whisky is derived. Then we come to American whiskies, which come in two main forms: Bourbon and rye. Bourbon must be made in the United States (the state of Kentucky is believed to be the birthplace of this form of American whiskey) and must be made using a grain mixture which is at least 51% corn. Bourbon is also made using a sour mash process, and aged in charred new oak barrels. In America, rye is made using a mash made from no less than 51% rye, and like bourbon, rye is aged in charred new oak barrels. Generally speaking, corn-based bourbon has a sweeter flavor, while rye is on the drier side. But as with all whiskies, there are so many varieties and factors that influence the flavor, it's a complex category. Within the Scotch category alone there are the famed peaty whiskies from the isle of Islay that have a distinctly smoky flavor, due to the process of drying the malted barley over peat-heated fires. In Japan, they spell whisky the Scottish way, and in broad terms, Japanese whisky is more similar to Scotch than any other style of whisky. Whisky connoisseurs all have their favorites — and a good bartender will be able to recommend a whisky variety to suit your tastes. Now have some fun with these recipes and get to know your bourbon from your rye and your Scotch from your whiskey.

Photography by: PhotC

The Dunmore Pineapple

CREATED BY *Chris Chamberlain*

Lead Mixologist at Elixir Craft Cocktails, and National Beverage Development Manager at E&J Gallo Spirits

INGREDIENTS

- 1 ounce Jura Superstition whisky
- 1 ounce New Amsterdam pineapple vodka
- ½ ounce fresh pressed lime juice
- ½ ounce homemade tropical orgeat syrup *(Pg. 190)*
- 3 ounces East Imperial Mombasa ginger beer
- Pineapple fronds, and a dried pineapple ring, dusted with powdered sugar, for garnish

DIRECTIONS

Add the ingredients into a copper mug, and stir together with a bar spoon. Top the mixture off with crushed ice, and garnish with a couple of pineapple leaves and a dried pineapple ring, dusted with powdered sugar.

INSPIRATION

I was traveling through Scotland, exploring the idea of Scotch, and I cam across this obscure building, called the Dunmore Pineapple, that has this huge pineapple-shaped cupola on top of it. The juxtaposition of having pineapple and tropical identity in the north sea of Scotland just seemed so obscure to me, so it seemed like a great inspiration for a Moscow Mule.

Chris **Chamberlain**   /chris.chamberlain.7545    @cchamberlain23   @elixircraftcocktails

Chris Chamberlain is an award-winning craftsman located outside the Philadelphia area. With more than two decades of hospitality and professional spirits industry experience, he has worked tirelessly in moving the craft of bartending forward. A graduate of the Beverage Alcohol Resource program, he also holds a Certified Spirits Specialist certification from the Society of Wine Educators. Not only a member of the USBG for 7-plus years, Chris has also served on the Philadelphia chapters council. In addition to his continued efforts to help develop, train, and educate those in the industry, Chris has achieved multiple accolades including many for his efforts in the WSWA Call for Cocktails competitions, and a win at the 2013 Iron Mixologist competition. His cocktails have been featured in various trade and media publications, and he has conducted cocktail seminars at such events as the world renowned Epcot Food & Wine Show.

Buck@ Mist

CREATED BY *Guido Sardi*

Beverage Manager, The Clubhouse, Sydney, Australia

INGREDIENTS

- 1 ½ ounces Bulleit Rye whiskey
- 1 ½ ounces Stone's Original Green Ginger Wine
- 2 ½ ounces yuzu juice soda *(Pg. 184)*
- ½ ounce ginger-agave nectar *(Pg. 185)*
- 3 drops cherry bitters
- 2 shiso leaves and a mezcal-soaked cherry, for garnish

DIRECTIONS

Combine the ginger-agave nectar and ginger wine in a shaker and stir without ice until well mixed. Add the rye whiskey and ice and shake until well chilled. Then strain into a copper mug filled with a few cubes of ice, and top up with the yuzu soda. Fill up the mug with crushed ice, and dash three drops of cherry bitters on the surface of the drink. Garnish with two shiso leaves and a mezcal-soaked cherry, and serve.

INSPIRATION

The name plays on the buck family of cocktails, and the more generally known bucket list. In this case a mist refers to the phenomenon where warm air (your hands) meets a sudden cooling (such as this category of drinks). My recent trip to Japan, and a bar manager role I held in a Japanese cocktail bar and restaurant, played a decisive role in the creation of this concoction.

Guido **Sardi**

 /Gigi.spinningtop @guido_sardi

Guido Sardi is an Italian bartender who has been living in Sydney, Australia since 2010. He began working in hospitality at the age of 20, and instantly fell in love with the bar world, due to the creativity it required and the opportunities it offered to travel and interact with different people each day. Guido often finds inspiration for his cocktail creations in childhood experiences — from his mamma's cooking to a fragrance that evokes a pleasant memory. What drives him every day is his passion for the craft of bartending, and the values ingrained in him by his parents, which include a great respect for mother nature. Guido is currently managing The Clubhouse, a cocktail bar and restaurant in Sydney, where he is gaining the skills necessary to realize his dream — his own cocktail bar.

Photography by: Hyku D Photograp

Farmer Elijah's Creole Mule

CREATED BY *Rebecca Sturt*

Consultant at Pineapple, Dubai, United Arab Emirates

INGREDIENTS

- 1 ½ ounces Elijah Craig Small Batch bourbon
- ½ ounce Ruby Port
- 1 ¼ ounces fresh carrot juice
- 1 ounce fresh orange juice
- ½ ounce fresh lime juice
- ¾ ounce fresh red bell pepper, ginger and chili syrup *(Pg. 185)*
- Splash East Imperial Mombasa ginger beer
- Garnish: 1 buttered Cajun baby corn cob, 1 baby carrot, 1 slice of fresh ginger, 1 red chili, half a small lime and a sprinkle of Louisiana Cajun Seasoning (Mix Cajun seasoning, crushed mixed peppercorns, and coarse sea salt with a hint of lime zest to create a fine powder).

DIRECTIONS

Build in a mixing glass, stir with hard ice for 20 seconds, and then double strain into a copper mug over cut or cubed ice. This drink is easy to batch and store chilled and then pour over fresh ice. Garnish with buttered Cajun baby corn, baby carrot, lime wheel, fresh ginger, red chili, and a sprinkle of Louisiana Cajun Seasoning.

INSPIRATION

My inspiration for this cocktail came from my love of making drinks with vegetables, and a recent visit to New Orleans. I wanted to create an easygoing and slightly healthy cocktail, made with fresh ingredients available year round. I chose Elijah Craig Small Batch Bourbon for its full flavor and bold finish, and because it also works well with vegetables, especially red bell peppers and spices like ginger. I took myself off to a local farm to find some fresh produce, and as Elijah Craig was a farmer I thought this was fitting. I love red bell peppers, and they are readily available around the world, as well as being rich sources of antioxidants and vitamin C. The ginger adds a hint of spice to complement the peppers, and is also one of the "must" components in a mule cocktail. I chose carrot and orange juice as they are a perfect match and a healthy drink on their own, and I found that they perfectly complemented the flavor of the port. Mules also eat carrots, which is another nice link back to the farm.

Rebecca **Sturt**

 Rebecca Sturt  @pineapplebc @pineapple_bar_consultancy

Rebecca began her career as a barback in 1995, and since then has never looked back. She has traveled the world, training and educating bartenders and sharing her love of the bartending craft for over 21 years. Over the years as a trainer and ambassador, she has educated and inspired more than 10,000 bartenders. A bartender at heart, she has had the opportunity to work in some amazing countries, gaining inspiration and sharing her knowledge across London, Beirut, Singapore, Australia, Africa, Maldives and now the UAE. Arriving in Dubai in 2006, Rebecca helped pioneer the bartending scene. She built and ran the first dedicated bartender training facility in the UAE, a position she held for over nine years, and now she runs the Dubai Bartenders Club. Rebecca can also now be found running her own bar consultancy company, called Pineapple.

Buckaroo

CREATED BY *Josh Powell*

Bar Manager, Ember, London, United Kingdom

INGREDIENTS

- 2 ounces Bulleit bourbon
- 1 ounce orange and ginger syrup *(combine 10 ounces simple syrup and 3 ounces freshly squeezed orange juice, and 2 1/2 ounces Perfect Purée of Napa Valley ginger)*
- 1 dash absinthe
- Fever-Tree soda water

DIRECTIONS

Build the first three ingredients in a copper mug over ice and churn to mix. Top up with soda water to a three quarter level. Add more ice and fill the rest of the way, leaving about a finger's wash line. To garnish, add a large sprig of fresh mint, and an orange twist for aroma.

INSPIRATION

This drink is almost an amalgamation of a mule and a buck. Those two words reminded me of horses that used to carry goods and equipment in olden times. It then reminded me of my favorite childhood game, Buckaroo, which is where the name came from. In the game, each player adds an item to the toy horse, trying to avoid it bucking them all off.

Josh **Powell**

f /josh.j.powell.7 🐦 @manhattan_gold 📷 @manhattan_gold

Josh Powell has been bartending for the past seven years. He started out working in a nightclub at the age of 19, before falling in love with cocktails. Josh is originally from Wales, but now lives in London, where he is the Bar Manager at bar and restaurant Ember. As well as taking part in various cocktail competitions, Josh also writes for educational website *The Alcohol Professor*.

Rocky Mountain Mule

CREATED BY *Cori O' Connor*
Bartender, Smokin' Dave's BBQ and Taphouse, Longmont, CO

INGREDIENTS

- 2 ounces Tin Cup whiskey
- ½ ounce Leopold Bros Rocky Mountain Blackberry Liqueur
- ½ ounce fresh lime juice
- Ginger beer
- Lime wedge, candied ginger and fresh blackberry, for garnish

DIRECTIONS

Add first three ingredients to a copper mug. Fill with ice and top with ginger beer. Garnish with a lime wedge, candied ginger and a fresh blackberry.

INSPIRATION

The Rocky Mountain Mule is inspired by fresh mountain air and snow capped peaks. Great Colorado spirits like Tin Cup whiskey and Leopoldo Bros. blackberry liqueur really shine in this drink, and will give all those who try it a little taste of the Rockies.

Cori **O'Connor** f /coriocon, /smokindavesbbqlongmont @coriocon, @smokindavesbbqlongmont

Cori O'Connor is a bartender living and working on the Front Range in Colorado. Originally from Florida, she moved west three years ago, and that's when bartending began to shift from job to career. Cori loves crafting unique and exciting cocktails, and introducing the world of fine spirits to folks that have not yet been exposed to them. When not working behind the bar, Cori enjoys exploring Colorado with her spouse, Casey, and their two feisty pups, Grimm and Matisse.

Old Square Mule

CREATED BY *Denzel Heath*

Head Bartender, MMI Bar Academy, Dubai, United Arab Emirates

INGREDIENTS

- 1 ounce Rittenhouse straight rye
- 1 ounce La Quintinye Vermouth Royal Rouge
- 1 ounce Bitter Orange & Ginger Oleo-Saccharum **(Pg. 187)**
- 3 ounces NOLA blonde ale
- 2 dashes Angostura bitters

DIRECTIONS

Premix equal parts Rittenhouse straight rye whiskey, La Quintinye Vermouth Royal Rouge and Bitter Orange & Ginger Oleo-Saccharum, and keep the mixture chilled. Add the three ounces of the premix and three ounces of NOLA blonde ale over cubed ice, then cap with crushed ice. Add dashes of bitters. Garnish with dehydrated candied leftovers from the Oleo, or simply an orange slice.

INSPIRATION

I was compelled to create a cocktail that tells a story about the ethnic melting pot that is the French Quarter – or 'The Old Square' – of New Orleans, an area that we bartenders love so dearly. This cocktail brings together American, French and Carribean ingredients, and combines them with local NOLA products. The resulting drink is simple, refreshing and spicy.

Denzel **Heath**

@bartenderismymiddlename

Award-winning bartender Denzel Heath is a firm believer in the craft of hospitality. Hailing from South Africa, he has spent his most recent years traveling across Africa to share his passion for bartending with like-minded individuals. Currently he resides in Dubai, where he is head of the MMI Bar Academy. He is responsible for spirit education and bar consulting, and is also an ambassador for brands that fall under the Maritime and Mercantile International (MMI) portfolio. He has 16 years of bar experience, gained in New York, Florida and South Africa, and has managed Africa's largest training program, the Master Bar Academy. He has repeatedly been a global finalist in prestigious cocktail and bartending competitions, and due to his success in the competitive arena, has been appointed a judge in several cocktail competitions in South Africa, Dubai, Lebanon and Cyprus. As a guest bartender, he has enjoyed working behind the stick at some of the finest establishments in the world, including bars in London, Dubai, Greece and Amsterdam. When all is said and done, Denzel is happiest behind the bar, serving up drinks to the thirsty and the cocktail-enthused.

Derby Mule

CREATED BY *James Cleland*

Bartender, Uni Restaurant, Boston, MA

INGREDIENTS

- 2 ounces Bulleit bourbon
- ¾ ounce lemon juice
- ¾ ounce cinnamon syrup
- 1 dash Bitterman's Elemekule Tiki bitters
- 4-6 mint leaves
- Maine Root ginger beer

DIRECTIONS

Combine bourbon, lemon juice, cinnamon simple, bitters and mint leaves in shaker. Add ice and shake. Strain over crushed ice in mule mug. Fill with ginger beer and garnish with mint.

INSPIRATION

A marriage of the Mint Julep and the Moscow Mule as a Kentucky Derby special. Two summer favorites in one!

James **Cleland**

[📷] @pegasuspaladin, @uni_boston

A bartender for the past six years in a variety of different settings, James has always loved a challenge. Forever a fan of gently persuading guests to enjoy a drink that's outside of their comfort zone, he creates playful riffs on classics. He also firmly believes that the right ingredient can go a lot further than a lot of ingredients, and he prefers keeping recipes simple. James created the Derby Mule as a combination of all of these, and is excited to share this drink as a midway point between a light, easy drinking Moscow Mule, and a strong but still refreshing Mint Julep. In his free time, James enjoys spending time outside with his two miniature pinschers, and is always looking for his next creative challenge.

Smokey Donkey

CREATED BY *Laurentiu Dedu*

Bucharest, Romania

INGREDIENTS

- 2 ounces Jura Superstition single malt Scotch whisky
- ½ ounce yuzu juice
- ¼ ounce simple syrup
- Fever-Tree ginger ale, to top
- Lemon peel, for garnish

DIRECTIONS

Shake the first three ingredients with ice, then pour into a copper mug, over ice. Top up with the ginger ale, and then garnish with lemon peel.

INSPIRATION

My inspiration was the Asian-themed venue where I work, and this culture's tendency to strive for perfection. The name comes from a blend of the smokiness of the Scottish whisky, and the fact that the word "ass" was out of the question!

Laurentiu **Dedu**

 /dedu.laurentiu @laurentiu_dedu

Laurentiu Dedu is a 30-year-old bartender from Bucharest, Romania. He is now a manager in one of the biggest club and bar groups in Bucharest. His career behind the bar started more than 12 years ago, as a barback. Then he attended bartending schools in Bucharest, and his ambition led him to London, where he graduated from the renowned European Bartender School. He created a Facebook group for bartenders called Bucharest Bartender Exchange, where he promotes bartending jobs and shares cocktail recipes. He occasionally teaches flair and mixology, and hopes to become one of the best in this arena.

Take Root

CREATED BY *Zachary Faden*

Bartender, Washington D.C.

INGREDIENTS

- 1 ½ ounces Monkey Shoulder whisky
- ½ ounce Linie aquavit
- 4 ounces ginger-carrot soda *(Pg. 189)*
- Fried, ginger-carrot tops *(Pg. 189)*

DIRECTIONS

Fill mule mug with one ounce of the soda. Add Monkey Shoulder whiskey and Linie aquavit, and then fill with ice. Top with soda. Add a straw, stir the drink, then top with the fried carrot tops garnish, serve, and enjoy!

INSPIRATION

The mule is a fantastic and refreshing introduction to the savory side of cocktails. I continue this tradition and make a drink marrying the beautiful flavor combination of ginger and carrot. Also, while prep-heavy, the finished Take Root stays true to the simplicity of the mule. The key ingredient of the classic mule is ginger. This cocktail embraces and emphasizes the fragrant zestiness of fresh ginger root. Ginger's earthiness is complemented by Monkey Shoulder whisky's mild smoke and spice, Linie aquavit's caraway and herbal notes, and is rounded out by carrot's brightness and natural sweetness. The result is a reinvigorating sipper.

Zachary **Faden**

  @SpiritsCurator

Zachary W. Faden was raised in the suburbs of Philadelphia and moved to the nation's capital to study history and philosophy at American University. He later studied in Scotland and completed his Masters in Intellectual History from the University of Edinburgh, before making D.C. his home. Following a career as a Department of Defense contractor, Faden's intellectual wanderlust had him applying his research skills and methodologies to his passion — the history and culture of drinking. His passion became a hobby, then an obsession, which in turn matured into a profession. Faden first trained at the James Beard Award-nominated D.C. cocktail bar Columbia Room, where he learned bar techniques and service etiquette. He later joined the James Beard Award-nominated bar program at Rogue 24, where he executed a cocktail program emphasizing chef-driven techniques. He then took on the role of bar manager and lead bartender at cocktail lounge Magnolia's on King in Alexandria, Virginia – further experimenting with drink research and development. Zachary has recently returned to the D.C. bartending scene, where he eventually plans to open his own bar.

Healing Mule

CREATED BY *Cagatay Zengin*

Bartender, Entwine Bar, New York, NY

INGREDIENTS

- 2 ounces Monkey Shoulder blended Scotch
- 2 slices of fresh ginger
- 1 ounce Amaro Montenegro
- ¼ ounce simple syrup
- ¾ ounce fresh lemon juice
- 1 ounce unsweetened cold black tea
- 1 ounce seltzer water
- Lemon wheel with ginger candy and mint leaves, for garnish

DIRECTIONS

Muddle the ginger slices finely, then add the Amaro Montenegro and the simple syrup, then vigorously dry shake. Add the rest of the ingredients — omitting the seltzer water— and hard shake for 15 seconds. Add the seltzer to the shaker and double strain it into the mug on a few one inch sized ice cubes. Garnish with lemon wheel with ginger candy and mint leaves.

INSPIRATION

I created this cocktail for my wife, who likes refreshing and easy-to-drink beverages. The combination of black tea and fresh ginger was one of the things that pushed me to create this drink, and the addition of Amaro Montenegro gave it perfect balance.

Cagatay **Zengin**

@drinkchemist

Originally from Turkey, Cagatay Zengin studied chemical engineering before moving NYC. He started to work at Entwine Bar as a cook, and then worked his way up to the role of bartender and shortly after became a mixologist. His passion is classic cocktails, but he also loves to create modernized versions. One of his great joys in life is being behind the bar and connecting with people in his adopted homeland of the Big Apple.

Kicking Mule

CREATED BY *Max Verrier*

Bartender, HIMKOK, Oslo, Norway

INGREDIENTS

- 1 1/3 ounces Bulleit bourbon
- 1 ounce carrot juice (fresh if possible)
- 1/3 ounces sugar syrup
- 1/3 ounces lime juice
- Fever-Tree ginger beer

DIRECTIONS

In a copper mug, pour all of the ingredients, except the ginger beer. Fill the mug up with cubed ice and top with ginger beer. Give it a quick stir and serve. Garnish with a lime wheel and a carrot wheel.

INSPIRATION

Inspired by one of our best selling cocktails at HIMKOK, the Beta Cocktail. It's a vodka drink with the fresh ginger juice, fresh carrot juice, Aperol infused with horseradish, lemon and sugar. Kicking Mule is an effective way to represent this drink with as little prep as possible, and with the bourbon kick! Cheers.

Max *Verrier*

Max Verrier is a 28-year old French bartender. At one time, he was a helicopter pilot in the U.S., until the fateful day he touched ground behind a bar in St. Tropez. That was eight years ago, when he held a cocktail shaker in his hand for the first time — and it has been there ever since. Max then spent the next few years bartending in various high-end restaurants, hotels and cocktail bars in France and London, teaching himself all that he knows today. One year ago, he received an incredible opportunity to go to Norway and be part of a new ambitious project — HIMKOK, the bar and distillery in Oslo where Max is currently mixing up his signature cocktails.

Bourbon Street Mule

CREATED BY *Scott Diaz*

Bar Manager, The Triple Door, Seattle, WA

INGREDIENTS

- 1 ½ ounces Bulleit bourbon
- ½ ounce Amaro Montenegro
- ½ ounce fresh lemon juice
- 12 drops 18.21 Chamomile bitters
- 4 ounces Gingeroo

DIRECTIONS

Pour the bourbon, Amaro Montenegro, lemon juice and bitters into a shaker tin over ice, shake and strain into an iced copper mug. Top with Gingeroo, garnish with a large swath of lemon peel, and enjoy.

INSPIRATION

This cocktail embodies the spirit of New Orleans, with its rich, vibrant and diverse culture. I believe cocktails should be simple, yet complex, and express one's love of the cocktail and those who craft them.

Scott **Diaz**

 @scottybarfly

Scott Diaz is an award winning cocktail and spirits professional with over 20 years of experience in the industry. His cocktails have been featured in prestigious publications such as *Cheers* magazine, *Stew Ellington's 901 Very Good Cocktails: A Practical Guide, Gaz Regan's 101 Best New Cocktails* (2013 and 2014), and *The Bartender's Bible* (11th Edition), by Simon Difford. Scott has competed in numerous cocktail competitions and in 2014 he was crowned co-winner of the first annual Kindred Spirit Competition, staged by *D* magazine and Glenfiddich whisky. That same year, he authored a Washington produced vermouth with local distillery, broVo Spirits. In 2015, The Beverage Institute awarded the broVo "Pink" rosé vermouth 93 points. Scott can currently be found running the beverage program and operations at Seattle's iconic music and theater venue, The Triple Door.

Rum Mules

Any mention of rum often conjures up images of tropical drinks, likely because the majority of the world's rum production occurs in the Caribbean and in Latin America. Although today, rum is produced in many nations across the globe, including Spain, Australia, New Zealand, South Africa, Taiwan, Thailand, Japan, the United States and Canada. Historically, this spirited beverage also has strong affiliations with the Royal Navy — where it was mixed with water or beer to make "grog." Rum is also closely associated with piracy, a prime example being the tipsy swashbuckler Captain Jack Sparrow in the Pirates of the Caribbean *movie franchise. So just what is rum? It is essentially a distilled alcoholic beverage made using the byproducts of sugarcane, such as molasses, or made directly from sugarcane juice, by a process of fermentation and distillation. The distillate, a clear liquid, is then often aged in oak barrels, giving it a darker color. Rums are produced in various grades — light rums are commonly used in cocktails, whereas golden and dark rums were typically consumed straight or neat, on the rocks, or used for cooking, but today all varieties of rum are becoming increasingly popular in cocktails. As you'll see from the following recipes, many of our bartenders replaced the vodka in a traditional Moscow Mule with rum, for an exotic take of the classic! Enjoy.*

Beet the Mule

CREATED BY *Shannon Stiggins*

Bar Program Director, The V Palm Springs, Elixir Bar and Solstice Restaurant, Palm Springs, CA

INGREDIENTS

- 1 ½ ounces Rhum Barbancourt
- ½ ounce Montelobos mezcal
- ½ ounce ginger syrup
- ½ ounce beet juice
- ¾ ounce lime
- Pinch of salt
- Fever-Tree ginger beer

DIRECTIONS

Shake Rhum, mezcal, ginger, beet, lime and salt. Then strain into charged mug. Garnish with a pina leaf, ginger candy and dehydrated lime wheel. Garnish with pina leaf, ginger candy and dehydrated lime wheel.

INSPIRATION

There's a pressed juice I love called Pink Punk that has ginger and beet in it, and I thought a mule variation with rum and mezcal would be amazing — healthy yet boozy!

Shannon **Stiggins**

[Instagram] @thatbleachedblonde

Throughout her stellar career, Shannon has been an integral team member at the launch of many upscale bars and restaurants. She began in the cocktail mecca of New York City, with stints behind the bar at Vero Uptown and Downtown, STK, and American Whiskey. She then landed the coveted head bartending position at Cosme, the first New York venture of famed restaurateur Einrique Olivera, whose Mexico City eatery Pujol won three Michelin stars. She also consulted on the expansion of Dylan's Candy Bar, where she developed and relaunched the cocktail program for the Upper East Side venue, and opened the chain's inaugural Chicago location. Shannon then helped launch the cocktail program at Ian Schrager's New York EDITION Hotel, before joining New York-based hospitality company Blank Slate Group to help them open three high profile projects. In April 2016, Blank Slate Group launched the new V Palm Springs Hotel, and their first of two food and beverage outlets in Palm Springs. The first was Elixir Pool Bar and Grill, with an innovative cocktail program under Shannon's direction. This preceded the October opening of the hotel's modern American restaurant and cocktail bar, Solstice. This is where Shannon has now created two Mediterranean-inspired cocktail programs that are garnering rave reviews and national media attention.

Grandpa Sam

CREATED BY *Emil Head*
Bartender, Svartengrens, Stockholm, Sweden

INGREDIENTS
- 1 ¼ ounces Gosling's Black Seal Bermuda black rum
- 2/3 ounce Pineau des Charantes
- 2 teaspoons Ancho Reyes chili liquor
- 1 ounce lime juice
- 2/3 ounce IPA syrup *(Pg. 185)*
- 2 dashes orange bitters
- Fever-Tree ginger beer, to top

DIRECTIONS
Add all ingredients, except the ginger beer, to a copper mule mug over ice. Top off with a splash of ginger beer, then garnish with a fresh mint sprig and half a grilled lime (grilled cut side down until golden brown).

INSPIRATION
My inspiration behind the Grandpa Sam cocktail was winter in Sweden — I wanted to create a drink with deeper, warmer flavors to reflect the colder, darker part of the year in Sweden, but to make a drink that was still refreshing.

Emil **Head**

 /emil.hed.359   @mr.e.hed

Emil Hed's life behind the bar took off four years ago, when he was living and working in Australia. There, Emil had the privilege to work as a barback with some truly inspiring and talented bartenders at Sydney's Shady Pines Saloon. After his craft cocktail awakening in Australia, Emil returned to Sweden, where he honed his expertise on classic cocktails, developed his creativity, and gained confidence in his newfound profession. Emil currently is mixing drinks at the award-winning cocktail bar at Stockholm's esteemed contemporary fine dining establishment Svartengrens. At Svartengrens, the approach to ingredients is super seasonal and local, and Emil says rediscovering what Sweden has to offer in terms of nature's herbs, fruits and berries is what drives him.

Haitian Mule

CREATED BY *Justyn Myers*

Bartender, The Interval, San Francisco, CA

INGREDIENTS

- 2 ounces Rhum Barbancourt white rhum
- 2 ounces brut cava
- ¾ ounce fresh lime juice
- ¾ ounce honey syrup
- 5 medium basil leaves
- 5 medium slices fresh young ginger

DIRECTIONS

Muddle fresh ginger with the lime juice, honey syrup and Rhum in a mixing tin. Add basil leaves, ice and shake. Add cava to tin and double strain everything into a mule mug over fresh ice. Garnish with a sprig of basil.

INSPIRATION

Basil, lime and ginger are a match made in heaven, and those flavors pair perfectly with the grassy funkiness of Rhum Barbancourt.

Justyn **Myers**

 @justynmyers

Justyn Myers discovered his passion for mixing cocktails in 2011, when he was unexpectedly put behind the bar at an art event. He is currently a bartender in San Francisco at The Interval at Long Now, a thoughtful craft cocktail bar and non-profit organization dedicated to long-term thinking. Myers also created the cocktail program for The Racket, a neo-noir murder mystery party game.

Double Barreled

CREATED BY *Kevin Feldman*

Bartender, Driftwood Kitchen / The Deck, Laguna Beach, CA

INGREDIENTS

- 1 ¼ ounces Ballast Point Three Sheets Barrel Aged Rum
- ½ ounce Deadhead 8 Year Aged Rum
- ½ ounce fresh squeezed lime juice
- ¼ ounce orgeat syrup
- 1 dash orange bitters
- ¼ ounce island coconut and ginger-infused tea *(Pg. 185)*
- Pineapple foam *(Pg. 185)*
- Cock'n Bull ginger beer, to top
- Whiskey barrel smoked papaya and spiced candied pineapple, for garnish

DIRECTIONS

Add both rums, lime juice, orgeat, infused tea and bitters into a shaker. Add ice and shake, then double strain into a copper mule mug. Top with a splash of ginger beer, and the pineapple foam, then garnish with a slice of whiskey barrel smoked papaya and some spiced candied pineapple.

INSPIRATION

The concept of the Double Barreled came to me while sitting on a surfboard, waiting for the next set of waves to come through. The ultimate thrill for any surfer is finding the perfect wave, to form a barrel. Getting "barreled" by a wave only occurs when all the elements of Mother Nature coincide at just the right point. Inspired by the spirit of the sea, I wanted to incorporate the process and patience of a barrel-aged rum with the balance of tropical ingredients, to create a cocktail that pays homage to the 1941 classic mule, while allowing the drinker to transcend into their own "double barrel."

Kevin **Feldman**

@feldman.kevin

Raised in the South Florida, Kevin's career began as a barback, a position that helped him build a foundation and ignite his passion for the bar scene. After spending four years in the navy, he moved to Chicago and started tending bar in the vibrant Wrigleyville neighborhood surrounding the Cubs ballpark. After six years in Chicago, Kevin relocated to Laguna Beach, California, to serve up some good vibes by the sea. His experiences of both city life in Chicago and beach life in California have helped him to develop his crafting style, and can be reflected in his cocktail creations.

Photography by: coltandpatie

Red-Eyed Buck

CREATED BY *Elysha Rose Diaz*

Bartender, Q&C Hotel Bar, New Orleans, LA

INGREDIENTS

- 1 ½ ounces Don Q Cristal rum
- ½ ounce Pusser's Rum Original Admiralty Blend (Blue Label)
- 1 ounce cardamom-infused simple syrup *(Pg. 188)*
- ¾ ounce freshly squeezed lime juice
- ¼ ounce fresh ginger juice *(in a masticating juicer, juice a large chunk of fresh ginger)*
- 3 dashes pure vanilla extract
- 3 ounces Carbonated Highwalk Blend Cold Brew Coffee (courtesy of Congregation Coffee Roasters) *(Pg. 188)*
- Wide lime twist, for garnish

DIRECTIONS

In a cocktail shaker filled with ice, combine: rums, simple syrup, lime juice, ginger juice, and vanilla extract. Shake well to chill. Strain into an ice-filled copper mug. Top with the carbonated coffee. Garnish with a wide lime twist and serve with a straw or a stir stick.

INSPIRATION

The inspiration behind this bright, gingery cold brew buck is threefold: Cajun red-eye gravy, fresh ginger juice, and hot, humid Louisiana summer nights.

Elysha Rose **Diaz**

@congregationola @congregation_coffee

Elysha Rose Diaz is a craftsperson at heart. While her artwork ranges from large wooden furniture to tiny knit toys – with all things paper, leather, and fabric in between – for the past 15 years she has traded her arts, crafts and parenting days for nights in the high-energy atmosphere of restaurants and craft cocktails. Currently, Elysha handles the cold brew and coffee cocktail R&D for Congregation Coffee Roasters, while running social media and brand management for the company.

The Carrot and Stick Approach

CREATED BY *Torrence O'Haire*

Wine Director & Experience Specialist, The Downtown Market Grand Rapids, Grand Rapids, MI

INGREDIENTS

- 1 ¼ ounces Pusser's Rum Gunpowder Proof
- ¾ ounce Barrow's Intense Ginger liqueur
- ¾ ounce fresh lemon juice
- ½ ounce fresh carrot juice
- ¼ ounce Monin pineapple syrup
- Approx. 2 ounces Fever-Tree Premium soda water (to fill glass)
- 2 dashes Bittercube Blackstrap bitters

DIRECTIONS

Combine the first five ingredients in a cocktail shaker and fill with ice. Shake very well, until foamy and well-chilled. Strain over large cubes in a copper mug and top with soda water to fill. Stir gently, and dash bitters over the surface of the drink.

INSPIRATION

I started composing this drink from a culinary standpoint — what sorts of things do I like to do with ginger when I'm cooking? I threw a dinner party once where I made a salad of shaved carrot, fresh ginger, and fresh pineapple, topped with a brown sugar-cumin vinaigrette and it was a smash hit on a stormy summer evening. Combining the "summer storm" cocktail-hour (where the drinks should be both refreshing and conversation-starting, as you're stuck indoors) with the basic idea of that recipe began my conceptualization of this cocktail. The name refers to the challenge some bartenders have in selling overproof spirits regularly. By "luring" the novice bar guest with the sweet, earthy, fragrant combination of carrot, pineapple, and spice, the burn of the ginger and the pop of the rich high-proof rum comes in with an exciting wallop that keeps one's mouth watering. Plus, when I think of a mule, I think of the carrot dangling from a string at the end of a long stick, encouraging the stubborn beast to keep moving. Even at my most stubborn, one of these will definitely keep me heading forward.

Torrence **O'Haire**

f /tohaire @bacchanology

Torrence (Tory) O'Haire is a chef, food writer, teacher, sommelier, spirits specialist, mediocre fencer, terrible poet, and gentleman adventurer currently raising hell with his charming partner in Chicago, Illinois. Having spent 17 years in the industry, he credits his love of food, drink, and hospitality to his Francophilic upbringing deep in the Michigan woods, where his family of cooks, artists, and farmers always knew how to set an extra place at the table, fill your glass, and tell a damn good story.

The Queen Elizabeth

CREATED BY *Buddy Newby*

Bartender, Tank House BBQ and Bar, Sacramento, CA

INGREDIENTS

- 1 ounce Pusser's Rum
- 1 ounce Pusser's Rum Gunpowder Proof
- 1 ounce lime juice
- 3 slices of ginger
- ¼ ounce honey syrup
- ¾ ounce grapefruit syrup
- 5 drops Bittercube Blackstrap bitters
- Fever-Tree club soda

DIRECTIONS

Muddle ginger with honey and grapefruit syrups. Add rum and lime juice. Then, ice shake and double strain into a copper mug filled with crushed ice. Add Blackstrap bitters and top with club soda. Garnish with a lime twist and a thinly sliced stick of fresh ginger.

INSPIRATION

The idea for this drink came from a take on naval grog. I used two types of British navy rum, and substituted the grapefruit juice for grapefruit syrup, to give it a sweeter taste. That sweetness also helps to balance out the higher proof rum. The name comes from an aircraft carrier that the British navy will be christening this year. It also occurred to me that a mule carries cargo — so the aircraft carrier was a fun play on that.

Buddy *Newby*

 @buddynewby

Buddy Newby is a 34 year-old who hails from Sacramento, California. He has been bartending for five years, after starting out at a local restaurant and working his way up from bus boy. He has been working at Tank House BBQ and Bar since its opening. As a rum and exotic cocktail enthusiast, he developed quite a following for his tiki drinks. So strong was this following, it inspired Buddy to join forces with the Tank House owners to open Jungle Bird in October 2016, a bar bringing tiki cocktails and island-inspired fare to midtown Sacramento.

Serpent and the Mule

CREATED BY *Jesse Carr*

Bar Director, Balise, New Orleans, LA

INGREDIENTS

- 1 ½ ounces Raisin Infused Rhum Barbancourt 8yr **(Pg. 188)**
- ½ ounce Giffard Bigallet China China liqueur
- ¼ ounce Giffard Vanille de Madagascar liqueur
- ¾ ounce lime juice
- ½ ounce pineapple juice
- ½ ounce ginger syrup **(Pg. 188)**
- Fever-Tree ginger beer

DIRECTIONS

Combine all ingredients, except ginger beer, in a shaker tin with ice, short shake (about 6-8 shakes), and then strain into a mule mug and add ice. Top with Fever-Tree ginger beer. Garnish with manicured pineapple skin hung on the rim, with three pineapple leaves inserted and enjoy.

INSPIRATION

The book *The Serpent and the Rainbow* inspired the name, while the actual flavors of the cocktail were inspired by the city of New Orleans and the great pineapple cakes that I have had here.

Jesse **Carr**

   @jessecarr328   @jessecarr328   @kidinfo

Raised along the eastern seaboard, from Georgia to Virginia where he was raised by mostly his grandparents, Jesse started the beginnings of learning what would later become his passion and career. Jesse's grandparents were true southerners, with a love of socializing and always believed that it was five o'clock somewhere. He would participate by playing bartender. After attending military school, he moved to California to attend college and stretch his legs. While at college, Jesse began bartending at local pubs and fond his fondness for hospitality. After some traveling he landed in New York, where he began working with some of the greatest talents in the industry. He found a home for the past three years at the James Beard Winner Maison Premiere, where he and his colleagues worked tirelessly to create one of the best bars in the world. Jesse has now moved to New Orleans, a city he fell in love many years ago, and is honored to be working with the great team at Le Petite Grocery and Balise.

Sub Recipes

Not-So Secret Ingredients

The talented mixologists who have helped us put together this book have also been generous enough to share with us some of their secret weapons — their handmade syrups, sodas, shrubs, infusions and more.

Aztec Mule

//////////////////////////////////// (Pg. 123)

Blueberry-Ginger Shrub:
Combine three ounces of puréed blueberries (with pulp), one cup white sugar, one ounce fresh squeezed ginger juice, and one and three quarter ounces of apple cider vinegar. Mix all ingredients, seal, and sous vide at 60 degrees Celsius (140 degrees Fahrenheit) for 45 minutes. Filter through a cheesecloth, and be sure to squeeze the blueberry pulp to extract maximum juice, before discarding the pulp.

Bangkok Buckshot

//////////////////////////////////// (Pg. 97)

Kaffir Lime and Lemongrass Water:
Boil a half an ounce each of kaffir lime leaves and chopped lemongrass with eight cups of water for around 20 to 30 minutes. Cool to room temperature, and strain.

Galangal Syrup:
Combine equal parts of juiced and strained galangal root with 2:1 parts demerara syrup.

Blackcurrant Mule

//////////////////////////////////// (Pg. 91)

Coriander Infused Vodka:
Combine 34 ounces of vodka and 1.7 ounces (around a quarter of a cup) of coriander seeds in a large glass jar or vessel. Cover, and leave for several days. Then strain out the coriander seeds, and pour the vodka into a bottle.

Blackcurrant Purée:
In a blender, mix together two cups of blackcurrants with two cups of simple syrup. Strain and pour into a bottle.

Blossoms On Silk Road

//////////////////////////////////// (Pg. 98)

Chai Ginger Syrup:
Brew one cup of chai tea. Add one cup of roughly chopped ginger and one cup of sugar. Blend together on high until ginger is puréed, and let sit until at room temperature. Then fine strain and bottle for refrigeration.

Buckaroo

//////////////////////////////////// (Pg. 148)

Orange-Ginger Syrup:
Combine 10 ounces simple syrup, three ounces freshly squeezed orange juice, and two and a half ounces of Perfect Purée of Napa Valley Ginger.

Buck@ Mist

//////////////////////////////////// (Pg. 144)

Yuzu Soda:
Add equal parts of yuzu juice and filtered water to a CO2 siphon and charge.

Ginger-Agave Nectar:
Simmer one ounce of peeled ginger for every 10 ounces of agave nectar for 20 minutes. Chill before use.

Chamomule
//////////////////////////////////// (Pg. 75)

Lemon Flower Garnish:
Using a channel knife, make eight vertical, equidistant peel lines going down the long side of a fresh lemon. Turn lemon on its side and slice lemon wheels as you normally would. This should give you some awesome flower/cog looking lemons. Lastly, use a paring knife to cut a semicircle right between the flesh and pith of the lemon, leaving the outer peel intact, This gives you a lip of lemon flesh that can be bent back into a serving glass that leaves the outer peel hanging off the edge of the glass.

Chamomile Syrup:
You'll need loose chamomile tea/flowers and clover honey. Bring four cups of water to gentle boil and add about one cup of chamomile tea/flowers and simmer for 10 minutes. Fine strain while still warm and add in a 1:2 ratio of honey (E.g. Four cups of tea to two cups of honey). Let cool, and then bottle.

Double Barreled
//////////////////////////////////// (Pg. 174)

Island Coconut and Ginger-Infused Tea:
Boil up one cup of black tea, adding slices of fresh coconut and ginger to the mixture, for two minutes. Chill before use.

Pineapple Foam:
Dry shake one egg white and several chunks of muddled pineapple, until it forms a foam.

Duke of Orleans
//////////////////////////////////// (Pg. 59)

Ginger-Pineapple Shrub:
Add equal parts by weight of peeled ginger, pineapple, white wine vinegar and castor sugar. Bring to a boil, reduce and simmer for 30 minutes. Strain. Chill before use.

Farmer Elijah's Creole Mule
//////////////////////////////////// (Pg. 147)

Bell Pepper, Ginger & Chili Syrup:
Combine 16 ounces water with one cup of superfine sugar in a saucepan. Chop up three medium sized red bell peppers, one small red bird's eye chili (ends cut off) and two one-to-one-and-a-half inch pieces of fresh ginger. Add to the saucepan, bring close to the boil, then reduce and simmer for 20 minutes. Allow to cool before straining the liquid. Once strained, bottle and chill before use.

Grandpa Sam
//////////////////////////////////// (Pg. 170)

IPA Syrup:
Combine two cups (16 ounces) of IPA beer – the more hops, the better – with two cups of sugar in a saucepan. Let simmer for about 30 minutes, or until the liquid thickens to a syrup-like consistency. Chill before use.

Grant's Mule
//////////////////////////////////// (Pg. 63)

Wild Hibiscus Tea Syrup:
Combine eight ounces of hot water and eight ounces of demerara sugar, and add five wild hibiscus tea bags. Steep until room temperature. Remove bags and transfer to a fridge-safe storage container.

Hakka Mule
/////////////////////////////////// (Pg. 131)

Chinese 5 Spice Ginger Beer:
Combine two ounces fresh ginger juice, four ounces lemon juice, six ounces Chinese 5-Spice Simple Syrup (see recipe below), and 20 ounces cold water. Pour into a CO2 siphon and charge.

Chinese 5 Spice Simple Syrup:
Combine one cup granulated sugar, two cups water, two tablespoons honey, six star anise pods, two tablespoons fennel seed, two tablespoons Szechaun peppercorns (substitute green peppercorns if unavailable), one tablespoon whole cloves, and four three-inch cinnamon sticks (or two six inch sticks broken into pieces). Add spices to dry saucepan and heat over medium heat until fragrant (about three to four minutes). Add remaining ingredients and bring to a simmer. Simmer for 10 minutes, turn off the heat and steep for an hour. Strain and keep refrigerated for up to two weeks.

Just Beet It
/////////////////////////////////// (Pg. 102)

Ginger Syrup:
Combine equal parts juiced ginger root and sugar. Heat over medium-high heat, stirring to dissolve sugar. Chill before use.

Cinnamon Syrup:
Combine eight cinnamon sticks in a sauce pan with one cup of simple syrup and one cup of water. Boil, let cool, and then remove the cinnamon sticks. Chill before use.

King Palm Java Jenny
/////////////////////////////////// (Pg. 60)

Ginger-Coconut Shrub:
In a saucepan, combine one cup candied crystalized ginger, two cups unsweetened shredded coconut, one-and-a-half cups sugar, and three cups water. Stir over medium-high heat, then bring to a boil. Reduce heat and simmer for 20 minutes. Add two cups of champagne vinegar and simmer for 10 minutes more. Remove from heat and let cool completely before straining.

Marigny Mule
/////////////////////////////////// (Pg. 43)

Tarragon-Lime Syrup:
In a saucepan, boil one cup of water, add one cup of sugar and stir until sugar is dissolved. Add a few sprigs of tarragon and a couple of lime peels to the simple syrup and let sit for a few hours until the flavors have been released into the syrup. Remove the limes and tarragon from the simple syrup, and let cool or refrigerate.

Maui Mule
/////////////////////////////////// (Pg. 31)

Pineapple-Sage Shrub:
In a saucepan, combine one cup of pineapple juice with two sage leaves and three quarters of a cup of apple cider vinegar with three quarters of a cup of sugar. Let the sugar dissolve, and then cool.

Midtown Mule
/////////////////////////////////// (Pg. 87)

House Pineapple Ginger Syrup:
Combine eight ounces pineapple juice (bottled), 16

ounces orange juice (fresh or bottled) eight ounces lime juice (fresh), 16 ounces sugar, one large bunch of fresh basil (about 20 leaves with stems), eight ounces fresh ginger root (sliced lengthwise) and one and a half tablespoons high-quality vanilla extract (Massey's is preferred). Simmer all ingredients over medium heat for 20 minutes. Strain, reserving sliced ginger for garnishes. Allow to cool before bottling.

Miso Mule
////////////////////////////////////. (Pg. 88)

Coconut Miso Sugar Syrup:
To a non-reactive container, add 17 ounces of stock sugar syrup, one bar teaspoon of food grade coconut essence and four ounces of miso paste. Stir thoroughly to mix, then seal with an airtight lid. Leave for one hour, mixing two to three times throughout the process. Filter through muslin to remove solids. Bottle and reserve.

Mule as a Cucumber
////////////////////////////////////. (Pg. 35)

Black Pepper Syrup:
Heat half a cup of whole black peppercorns and two pinches of crushed red pepper flakes on medium high heat, and toast for 30 seconds, shaking often to prevent burning. Add one cup water and one cup sugar, stirring to combine. Reduce the heat to medium-low and cook for a few minutes until the sugar has dissolved, then remove from the heat. Cool to room temperature, then strain the syrup. Chill before use.

Ginger Syrup:
Peel and process fresh ginger root to make ginger juice. Add three parts sugar to two parts ginger juice and blend until smooth.

Oaxacan Mule
////////////////////////////////////. (Pg. 139)

Ginger Syrup:
Combine equal parts (by volume) ginger, sugar and water. Combine sugar and water and bring to a boil. Add chopped ginger and return to the boil. Then low simmer, uncovered, for 20 minutes. Strain out the ginger, bottle and refrigerate.

Old Square Mule
////////////////////////////////////. (Pg. 152)

Bitter Orange & Ginger Oleo-Saccharum:
Combine the skin of eight oranges, one cup of chopped fresh ginger and two cups of superfine sugar. Place all the ingredients in a tupperware container that can be sealed airtight for 24 hours. Shake it every so often if you can, to muddle the macerated content to release the oils and juices. After 24 hours, strain out the liquid from the solids. Dehydrate leftover solids to use as candied garnishes.

One Eared Stag Mule
////////////////////////////////////. (Pg. 36)

Lemongrass Tincture:
Combine six or seven ounces of overproof vodka, one ounce of lemongrass, and approximately one teaspoon of lime peel (no pith). Rapid infuse within a half liter iSi whipping siphon. Double charge with two N2O canisters, shaking between each dose of nitrogen. Shake and let stand for five minutes before straining.

Ginger Beer:
Combine six-and-a-half ounces of ginger (peeled and juiced, which should yield around five ounces of ginger juice), five ounces of lime juice, just under half a cup of sugar, and 20 ounces of water. Whip ingredients in

a bowl until thoroughly mixed. Strain all ingredients through a wet linen lined chinois conical seive strainer. Use a funnel to get all of the ingredients into a soda siphon, and then double charge. Shake between each dose of nitrogen.

Pacific Mule
//////////////////////////////////// (Pg. 132)

Pomegranate Hibiscus Shrub:
Heat 13 ounces pomegranate seeds, three ounces dried hibiscus petals, one and a half cups cane sugar, one cup apple cider vinegar and one cup water in a saucepan on medium to low heat for around 10 to 15 minutes, without bringing to a boil. Stir occasionally, and allow to cool once ingredients begin to blend well. Strain into appropriate container (glass is best), allow to cool to room temperature, and then refrigerate before use. Yields around three cups.

Paradise Mule
//////////////////////////////////// (Pg. 64)

Paradise Bitters:
Combine all bitters — four ounces of Angostura, eight ounces of Peychaud's and four ounces of Fee Bros. rhubarb — and add one cup of dry, loose leaf chamomile tea. Steep for two hours and double strain through a tea strainer. Decant back into one of the empty bitters bottles to use for serving.

Pedal Tone
//////////////////////////////////// (Pg. 113)

Hibiscus Infused Gin:
Add 15 bags of Wild Hibiscus Company wild hibiscus herbal tea to one full bottle of Aviation gin. Let soak for 90 minutes. Remove tea bags, and store the gin in sealed container.

Red-Eyed Buck
//////////////////////////////////// (Pg. 177)

Cardamom-Infused Simple Syrup:
Dissolve one cup raw sugar into one cup boiling water, and add 20 lightly crushed green cardamom pods. Steep and chill overnight. Strain, or not, and chill before use.

Carbonated Highwalk Blend Cold Brew Coffee:
Steep 12 ounces of coarsely ground coffee in seven cups of cold, filtered water for 16 hours. Strain through a paper coffee filter or chinois. To carbonate, use one cartridge in an iSi soda siphon, following manufacturer's instructions (while ignoring the manufacturer's instructions to only use water).

Serpent and the Mule
//////////////////////////////////// (Pg. 182)

Ginger Syrup:
Combine one part ginger juice and one part sugar, and heat until sugar dissolves. Chill before use.

Raisin Infused Rhum:
Add half a cup of raisins to one 25 ounce bottle of of Rhum Barbancourt 8 year. Place in an iSi. Shake, charge with CO2 and shake again. Let sit for five minutes and then slowly let all the pressure out and strain off the Rhum.

Sichuan Mule
//////////////////////////////////// (Pg. 32)

Spiced Pineapple Juice:
In a large saucepan, combine 10 ounces of pineapple juice, one bar spoon green Sichuan peppercorns, one bar spoon red Sichuan peppercorns, four pieces dried chili, one piece black cardamom, 35 pieces white

cardamom, four pieces star anise, four slices licorice root, two cinnamon sticks, seven slices dried ginger, and 20 cloves. Heat gently, without bringing to a boil, for around 10 minutes. Chill before use.

Summer and Smoke
// (Pg. 67)

Smoked Peach Nectar:
Place 15 pounds of peaches, deseeded and cubed into one inch pieces, and half a cup superfine sugar, in a double boiler for four hours. Cool in an nice bath, then hickory smoke using a smoke gun.

Basil Infused Vodka:
Add 12 ounces Ketel One vodka and six basil leaves into an iSi soda siphon, nitrous whip, allow to rest for one minute, nitrous whip again, stand for one minute, then shake vigorously. Expel gas into shaker tin, unscrew and conical strain the basil from the vodka. If you don't have a soda siphon, this basil vodka can also be made through infusion. Simply combine a bunch of basil, washed and dried, and a liter of Ketel One vodka in a glass container. Store in a cool dark place, stirring occasionally, for three days, then conical strain the basil from the vodka

Take Root
// (Pg. 159)

Ginger-Carrot Soda:
Using a juicer, juice 28 ounces fresh carrot juice and four ounces fresh ginger juice. Strain through chinois, cheesecloth or nut-milk bag. Fill iSi soda canister and charge once with a CO_2 cartridge (include a pinch of fleur de sel).

Fried, Ginger-Carrot Tops Garnish:
Microplane fresh ginger root. Mix with an equal amount of sugar and a pinch of fleur de sel. Fry carrot tops. Remove carrot tops from the fryer and place on paper towels. Dust carrot tops with the ginger and sugar mixture.

The Burgundian Muildier
// (Pg. 79)

Almond Clove Ginger Cocoa Rye Soda:
Toast one and a half tablespoons of cloves and two tablespoons of caraway seeds in a saute pan. In a blender, add toasted clove and caraway seeds, plus around one teapsooon fresh ginger, four tablespoons dark Dutch cacao powder, three cups orgeat syrup, and two cups water. Blend, then fine strain, and chill. Then grab an iSi soda siphon, and follow these steps:

1. Insert the wide measuring tube into the bottle. Fill the siphon with the soda mixture. If the soda mixture is cold when poured in, and the siphon is kept in a cool place, then the soda water will be extra fizzy!

2. Insert the riser tube with gasket into the bottle through the measuring tube. Screw the siphon head onto the bottle so that it is straight and tight.

3. Insert an original iSi soda charger into the charger holder and screw the charger holder with inserted charger onto the soda siphon head until you can hear that all the contents of the charger have flowed in.

4. Shake the soda siphon vigorously at least five times. Then remove the empty iSi soda charger.

5. Gently press the lever to dispense the soda. Direct the stream toward the internal wall of the drinking vessel. Shake the soda siphon again if necessary, in order to ensure optimum flow.

The Cure to Being a Mule

// (Pg. 51)

Turmeric-Galangal Sweetener:

Shred fresh equal parts galangal and turmeric (around half a cup). If you can't find galangal, subsitute fresh ginger. Place the shredded ginger in glass or plastic jar with a lid. Add a quart of sugar, mix well and store in the fridge for two days. Take out of the fridge and add one quart of hot water. Stir the mixture until all of the sugar granules have melted. Pass the sweetener through a fine strainer, chill, and enjoy adding it to your cocktails.

Cinnamon Tincture:

Put a dozen whole cinnamon sticks into a quart-sized glass or plastic jar, and fill with high proof neutral spirit. Sit in a cupboard for at least a week. Pour into an atomizer, and prepare to impress your guests with cocktail theater.

The Dunmore Pineapple

// (Pg. 143)

Homemade Tropical Orgeat:

Soak two cups of sliced raw almonds (not salted or blanched) in water for 30 minutes. While almonds are soaking, cut one banana into slices, and sautee/brulee in a sauce pan with butter, and one ounce of E&J VSOP brandy. Once caramelized, remove and allow to cool. After 30 minutes, strain almonds and add to a food processor with the caramelized banana slices. Pulverize into a breadcrumb-like consistency. Add two cups of this mixture to a fresh bowl, with two and a quarter cups of fresh water. Let sit for four to six hours, stirring occasionally. After time has elapsed, double strain out the liquid into a fresh saucepan. Add a sliced Madagascar vanilla bean, one ounce of E&J VSOP brandy, a teaspoon of orange flower water, and

two cups of sugar. Stir the mixture on a low heat until all ingredients combine. Double strain the now created orgeat into a container, and allow to cool before use.

The Elit Mule

// (Pg. 92)

Jeffrey Morgenthaler's House-Made Ginger Beer:
1 ounce ginger juice (see notes below)
2 ounces fresh lemon juice, finely strained
3 ounces simple syrup
10 ounces warm water (cold if using the soda siphon)

First, peel and juice your ginger. I find that 1 ½ ounces of fresh ginger tends to work out to roughly an ounce of ginger juice. I recommend using a juicer if you're planning on making this often, otherwise use a microplane grater and fine strain the grated ginger through a cheesecloth to avoid any chunks in the final product.

You have two options for carbonating your ginger beer: you can ferment it in the bottle, or you can carbonate on-the-fly with an iSi soda siphon. While the soda siphon is easier to use, for the sake of authenticity you might want your ginger beer fermented in the bottle. The base recipe above will make one 16-ounce bottle of ginger beer, so if you're using the bottle brewing method, simply multiply the proportions by the number of bottles you will be using. If you're going the siphon route, note that the canister will hold 32 ounces of ginger beer. So simply double the batch.

Mix ingredients together. If using a soda siphon, pour ingredients into the canister, screw on lid, charge with CO_2, shake once, and refrigerate. You're done.

If you're planning on brewing in the bottle, I recommend using 16-ounce "EZ" flip-top bottles. You can find these on the internet, at a craft store, or at any homebrewing supply place. Next, find some wine yeast. I use Red Star Premier Cuvee champagne yeast. Fill each bottle with 16 ounces of your mixture and add roughly 25 granules of champagne yeast. Seal the cap securely, shake well, and store for 48 hours – no more, no less – in a warm, dark place. After 48 hours have passed, refrigerate immediately to halt the process. When the bottles are chilled, crack one open, mix up a mule and enjoy!

The Good Ship Liefde

(Pg. 27)

Shiso Ginger Syrup:

Bring 16 ounces water and 35 ounces sugar to a boil, add six to eight shiso leaves (with stems) and simmer for 10 mins. Place in a blender and liquefy. Fine strain and store in a refrigerator.

The Pistachio Mule

(Pg. 68)

Pistachio Infused Vodka:

Steep 20 to 30 unsalted, raw pistachios (with shells) in a liter of your favorite vodka. (We prefer Reyka.) Nuts can be added directly to the bottle. Add a dash of Bakto Flavors Pistachio Extract. Let steep overnight or longer for best results.

The Wandering Mule

(Pg. 57)

Hibiscus Bud-Infused Vodka:

To one liter of vodka, add two cups of whole, dried hibiscus flowers (or one cup if using cut, dried hibiscus flowers). Let infuse for 30 minutes. Strain the infused vodka into a clean bottle.

Zinger Meets Mezcal

(Pg. 136)

Hibiscus Ginger Soda Recipe:

To make, obtain an iSi soda siphon. Combine one liter of water, three quarters of a cup of sugar, six to seven hibiscus flowers, and one medium piece of ginger (peeled and cut in a medium dice, or smashed for better results). Add the water into a pot with the sugar, hibiscus flower, ginger and heat on high. After it comes to a boil, bring the heat down to to medium leave it there for 15 minutes. Remove, and then strain into a container and leave it at room temperature until it cools down. Once the mixture has cooled, pour it into a soda siphon with one charge of CO_2 and it will be ready to use.

Ginger Beer

A Ginger Beer Primer

Brewed ginger beer is an essential element of the classic Moscow Mule, adding that effervescence and spiciness that helps make this such a flavorful and distinctive drink. Today, there are plenty of varieties of ginger beer available, from sweet and spicy to citrusy, cloudy, craft concentrates or even downright boozy. When made just right, you will experience a bold ginger kick accompanied by fresh aromatics. Curious to learn more how ginger beer plays a critical role in pulling together the classic ingredients of a Moscow Mule? Read our Copper Science sections found on pages 10-13 and 224-233.

Spicy

Considered to be more of an artisanal style variety, **Q Ginger Beer** is crafted with quality ingredients and lower sugar levels than most. Made with real ginger and cloudy in appearance, Q packs the biggest ginger punch and lasts down to the last sip. In addition to the ginger, you will also be able to pick up notes of organic agave, a touch of coriander, cardamom, cayenne, rose oil, and orange peel. **Cock'n Bull Ginger Beer**, originally developed by Jack Morgan, owner of the renowned Cock'n Bull Restaurant in Hollywood, the home of the original Moscow Mule, is still available today. The English-style ginger beer features a distinctive, spicy flavor thanks to the ginger root extract.

Strong & Bold

The classic Reed's **Jamaican-Style Ginger Beer** is sweet but on the spicier side, with a strong ginger flavor that really packs a punch. Reed's has become very popular and expanded its product selection over the years, and now offers varieties that include a less sugary alternative as well as an extra spicy bold brew for those who really like their mules with a strong, spicy punch. Crafted using spring water and natural ingredients, **Llanllyr Source Fiery Ginger Beer** is a premium ginger beer made with gingers and spices that combine for an earthy base with a bold but balanced kick of spice.

Sweet

The traditional **Bundaberg Ginger Beer** is a popular classic that is brewed in barrels in Australia. This ginger beer is housed in distinctive, stubby brown glass bottles with a tear-off metal lid. It is on the sweet side, with a just a hint of ginger spice, and features the standard level of carbonation you'd expect from a mixer. Another sweet alternative is **Gosling's Ginger Beer** that has a hit of mild spice but ultimately finishes on a very sweet note.

Tangy

A line of artisanal, premium mixers out of the UK, **Fever-Tree's Ginger Beer** is as elegant as it is exceptional, making it the ginger beer of choice for many of the talented bartenders who shared their recipes with us in this book. Fever-Tree is made using two different types of ginger — a fresh, citrusy green ginger from Ecuador and a hot, earthy variety with origins in Nigeria. This gives the drink a uniquely balanced flavor profile, one that is spicy or tangy without being too peppery. The cloudy nature of the beer and the golden pieces of ginger floating towards the bottom of each bottle add to the authenticity and artisanal charm of this particular product.

Cloudy

While the aforementioned Fever-Tree and Q products tend to be on the cloudy side, another variety with cloudy credibility is **Seabold Ginger Beer**. Handcrafted in small batches in Los Angeles, Seabold really puts the ginger front and center. It is the color of ginger juice, and very lightly carbonated. Each batch is hand made and even individually numbered. When they sell out, that's it — there's no more until the next batch is cooked up. Available primarily in the Los Angeles area at farmers markets and juice stores, this is the closest you can get to homemade ginger beer without whipping up a batch in your own kitchen.

Fizzy

Stoli, the makers of premium vodka from the house of Stolichnaya, have capitalized on the popularity of the Moscow Mule, and now also sell their own branded **Stoli Premium Mixer Ginger Beer**. It is sold in four-packs of slim, elegant cans. Made with pure cane sugar, this offering can be described as well-balanced, with a spicy sweetness and nice carbonation level for those who enjoy their mules on the fizzy side.

Boozy

In the UK, they brew their ginger beer with an extra kick, in the form of alcohol. Boozy varieties include Crabbie's, whose **Crabbie's Original Alcoholic Ginger Beer** offers the additional boost of 4.8% alc/vol. Described by the company as "a refreshing, light-bodied ginger beer with a spicy fresh ginger flavor, notes of citrus and a warming finish," this beverage is a dreamy companion to any mule. Similarly, Fentimans, an artisanal soda company from the United Kingdom that has been around since 1905, brew up a boozy variety as well as a traditional non-alcoholic ginger beer. Their **Hollows and Fentimans All Natural Alcoholic Ginger Beer** is brewed with botanicals and herbs, and is a popular choice for those who like their mules on the strong and flavorful side.

Craft Concentrate

For those who like to experiment on your own, you can either make your own ginger beer at home or use a ginger beer concentrate. Lucky for you, Top Hat Provisions based out of San Francisco has done just that. Their popular **Top Hat Ginger Beer** is a craft concentrate that features quality ingredients of organic ginger extract, organic evaporated cane juice, lemon juice, apple cider vinegar, citric acid & filtered water. While immensely popular at music festivals for their craft mule kegs, you can mix with sparkling water or club soda at home and strike the perfect balance of ginger and spice for your own taste.

A Little on Limes

Just a lime, you say? Here's a little history you can share while hand-squeezing lime juice for the perfect Moscow Mule, and some notes on flavor to help you decide which lime to choose.

A TALE OF TWO LIMES

Before we get into the flavor profiles of the two main lime competitors, we thought you might want to get to know them on a more personal level. **First, the key lime.** Not to point fingers, but this minxy little green ball has an age-old reputation for getting around. Originally from Persia, traders fell hard for its zesty nature, and brought it to North Africa and the Near East (think Turkey). There the lime cast its spell over Crusaders, who spirited the promiscuous fruit away to Palestine and Mediterranean Europe. By the time Columbus sailed, European sailors had discovered it's ability to stave off scurvy, and the fruit became a traveling companion on the voyage to Hispaniola (now known as Haiti). Spanish settlers, besmitten with its tart appeal, carried the lime to the Florida Keys, where it picked up its name in 1905. It's also known as the bartender's lime, which just goes to show the type of company it keeps. **Then there's the Persian lime**. The most widely sold today in the U.S., the homeland of this fruit is as cloudy as an unfiltered ginger beer; it may have begun in the same region as its cousin, the key lime, making its way via the Mediterranean to Brazil, and then California. Or it could have been a product of Florida, the largest producer of the varietal until Mexico got in the game. It's also known as a Tahiti lime, so there's that possibility. Whatever the origin, we know for certain that its bloodlines aren't pure. In fact, scientists guess that the Persian lime's seedless fruit and thornless tree are a result of a cross between a key lime and either a lemon or the larger, lumpier citron (we told you the key lime got around).

LIMING YOUR MULE

So which of these two contenders should go in your mule? Depends on the flavor profile you're after. If you're looking to add a little more of the old mule kick into your concoction, a key lime is the assertive way to go, with an acidic, tangy citrus bite that has slightly herbal undertones. If, on the other hoof, you're into a milder bite, the Persian is less bitter and more accessible to a broader range of palates (plus, its larger size produces a lot more juice).

LIKE LIME, LIKE MULE

Following in the lime's footsteps, the Moscow Mule has been making its way around the globe too. Spreading from its humble origins at the Cock 'n Bull in Los Angeles, it is now in the repertoire of bars from New Zealand to Quebec, Cuba to Brazil, Japan to Paris. And, quite aptly, Russia.

What role does the lime play in a Moscow Mule? Read about the lime's acidic properties that make your Moscow Mule really pop. Flip to pages 10-13, 224-233 to learn more!

Minute Mules

It's fun to impress your friends and fellow Muleheads with creative cocktails featuring innovative ingredients, homemade syrups and exotic fruits and liqueurs. And we can't wait to grab our copper mugs and shakers and get behind the bar to recreate some of the amazing cocktail recipes showcased here this book.

But let's face it, sometimes life is busy, and occasions for libations are spontaneous. When you only have a few moments to create a cocktail, turn to these Moscow Copper Co. Minute Mules™. Using simple, easy to find ingredients, these straightforward mule recipes offer slight variations on the flavors of a classic mule.

These Minute Mules™ are ideal for when the neighbors stop by for an impromptu barbecue. Or for those post-work evenings when you have a surplus of blueberries and a hankering for something a little stronger than a smoothie. Or perhaps it's just Taco Tuesday and those tortillas piled high with carnitas and salsa are calling out for some spicy cocktails as an accompaniment.

Introducing Minute Mules™ designed to be mixed up in mere minutes. And, of course, when served up in a Moscow Copper Co. mug, these mules are instantly impressive!

Original Mule

Moscow Copper Co. Original

CLASSIC
The classic Moscow Mule, just like Grandma Sophie used to make. This drink's well-balanced blend of effervescent ginger beer, fresh lime juice and quality vodka is refreshing, uplifting and utterly delicious. We think the Original Mule can be enjoyed at any time, for any occasion, big or small.

DIRECTIONS
Place ice into a Moscow Copper Co. mug and pour in the vodka. Squeeze in lime juice and top with ginger beer. Stir. Garnish with a wedge of lime, and enjoy, just as Grandma Sophie did.

Lime for Garnish

2 oz. Stoli Vodka

1/4 oz. Fresh Squeezed Lime Juice

6 oz. Ginger Beer

Pomegranate Mule

Moscow Copper Co. Original

FESTIVE

There's something distinctly festive about the vibrant red of pomegranate arils and the wintery green of a sprig of fresh rosemary — so we think this pomegranate mule is a great one to serve friends and family at any holiday celebration.

2 oz.
Stoli Vodka

DIRECTIONS

Place ice, vodka, pomegranate arils, POM juice and lime juice into a shaker and shake. Pour into a Moscow Copper Co. mug, fill with ginger beer and top with a Grand Marnier floater. Garnish with lime wheel, pomegranate arils and sprig of fresh rosemary.

Pomegranate
Arils

1 1/2 oz.
POM
Juice

5 oz.
Ginger Beer

1/2 oz.
Grand Marnier

1/4 oz.
Lime
Juice

Rosemary
Sprig

Peach Mule

Moscow Copper Co. Original

2 oz. Peach Flavored Vodka

SWEET & JUICY

With the addition of the juicy sweetness of a ripe peach, this variation of the mule is an ideal way to welcome the onset of summer. The cinnamon stick adds a delicate warmth and spiciness, and the addition of peach vodka and Grand Marnier makes this a slightly sweeter concoction than the original mule.

DIRECTIONS

Place ice, peach vodka (we like Deep Eddy or Stoli), a couple of fresh peach wedges and lime juice into a shaker and gently shake. Pour into a Moscow Copper Co. mug, fill with ginger beer and top with a Grand Marnier floater. Garnish with a lime wheel, fresh peach wedge and a cinnamon stick.

1/2 Fresh Ripe Peach

6 oz. Ginger Beer

1/2 oz. Grand Marnier

Lime & Cinnamon Stick for Garnish

4 oz. Lime Juice

GINGER BEER

Grand Marnier
LIQUEUR
ORANGE & COGNAC
PARIS FRANCE

STOLICHNAYA
ESTABLISHED 1938
Stoli Peachik
PEACH FLAVORED
PREMIUM VODKA

Tequila Mule

Moscow Copper Co. Original

 BOLD
With the addition of a good quality reposado tequila in place of the usual vodka, plus a touch of jalapeño and cilantro, this mule was designed to be the perfect accompaniment to a serving of your favorite tacos, or any Mexican cuisine. The addition of good friends and lively conversation make this a drink that tends to invite more than one round. Salud!

 DIRECTIONS
Place ice, tequila, lime juice, and a few slices of jalapeño into a shaker and shake. Pour into a Moscow Copper Co. mug, fill with ginger beer and top with Grand Marnier floater. Garnish with sliced jalapeño, ginger and lime on a cocktail stick, with cilantro.

1/2 oz. Fresh Squeezed Lime Juice

Sliced Jalapeno

Sliced Ginger Root

Cilantro

6 oz. Ginger Beer

2 oz. Tequila Reposado

1/2 oz. Grand Marnier

GINGER BEER

REPOSADO Tequila

Grand Marnier
LIQUEUR
ORANGE & COGNAC
PARIS FRANCE

Blueberry Mule

Moscow Copper Co. Original

SWEETY & TANGY
With the addition of tangy yet sweet fresh blueberries, and a splash of blueberry flavored vodka, this delicious mule variation evokes memories of summer fruit punch, home baked goods and so much more. The lime and mint, and of course the ever-present tang of the ginger beer, make this mule a great accompaniment to a summer barbecue, but if you have fresh blueberries on hand, it can be enjoyed whenever your heart desires.

DIRECTIONS
Place ice, Stoli Blueberi, lime juice and a few fresh blueberries into a shaker and gently shake. Pour into a Moscow Copper Co. mug and fill with ginger beer. Garnish by sliding fresh blueberries, sliced lime wheels and mint leaves onto a cocktail stick.

Handful of Fresh Blueberries

Mint and Sliced Lime, for Garnish

1/4 oz. Fresh Squeezed Lime Juice

6 oz. Ginger Beer

2 oz. Stoli Blueberi Vodka

Maker's Mule

Moscow Copper Co. Original

FOR EVERYONE
The inclusion of the rich, caramel smoothness of Maker's Mark bourbon whisky transforms this mule into a warm, wonderful variation of the original. The zestiness of the ginger beer pairs beautifully with the vanilla-tinged sweetness of the bourbon whisky, as does the traditional use of fresh lime juice. We recommend savoring one of these while enjoying invigorating discussions with whisky-loving friends.

DIRECTIONS
Place ice into a Moscow Copper Co. mug and pour in the Maker's Mark Whisky. Squeeze in lime juice and top with ginger beer. Garnish with a wedge of lime and enjoy.

1/4 oz. fresh squeezed Lime juice

Lime for Garnish

2 oz. Maker's Mark Whisky

6 oz Ginger Beer

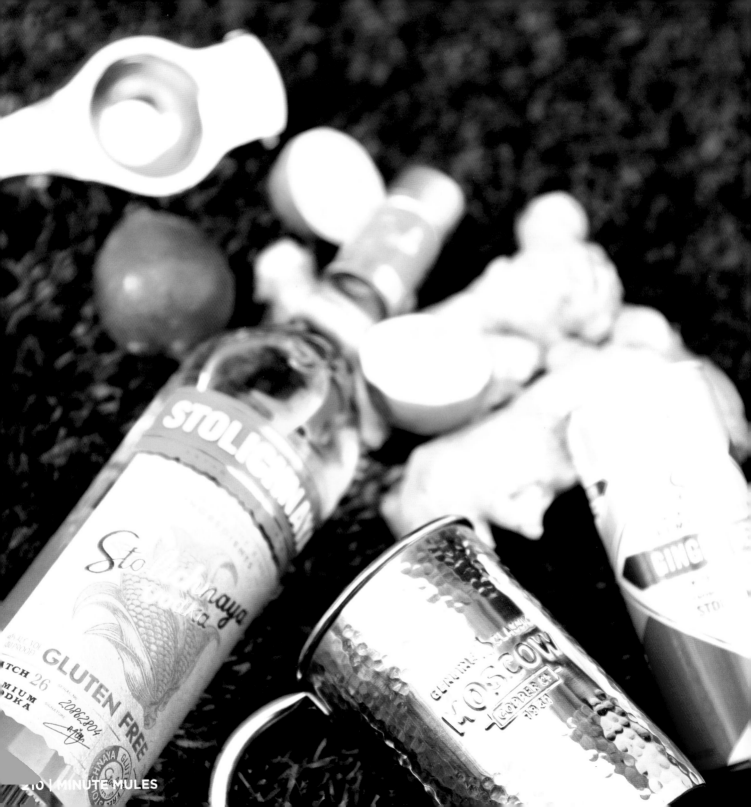

Gluten Free Mule

Moscow Copper Co. Original

FOR EVERYONE

With the growing number of people introducing gluten-free products into their lifestyles, it made sense for Stoli to develop a gluten-free vodka. Stoli's gluten-free vodka uses 88% corn and 12% buckwheat, so it's as smooth as you'd expect of such a quality vodka, but remains 100% gluten-free. Enjoy this traditional style mule as part of a gluten-free, Mulehead lifestyle!

DIRECTIONS

Place ice into a Moscow Copper Co. mug and pour in the Stoli Gluten Free vodka. Squeeze in lime juice and top with ginger beer. Garnish with a wedge of lime and enjoy.

1/4 oz. fresh squeezed Lime juice

Lime for Garnish

6 oz. Ginger Beer

2 oz. Stoli Gluten Free Vodka

Spicy Mule

Moscow Copper Co. Original

SPICY

For those who enjoy their flavors on the spicier side, the use of pepper flavored vodka and fresh chili peppers gives this mule a piquant kick, but the addition of cucumber cools things down, making this a rousing and refreshing drink all in one. We think this mule is a great alternative to a Bloody Mary at a weekend brunch.

DIRECTIONS

Place ice, pepper vodka, lime juice, a few slices of the peppers and cucumber into a shaker and shake. Pour into a Moscow Copper Co. mug, and fill with ginger beer. Garnish with sliced peppers, ginger, cucumber and lime on a cocktail stick.

2 oz.
Pepper Vodka

6 oz.
Ginger Beer

Fresh Sliced Cucumber

Sliced Jalapenas

Sliced Ginger Root

Sliced Red Chili Peppers

1/2 oz. Squeezed Lime Juice & Lime For Garnish

GINGER BEER

PEPPER VODKA

Skinny Mule

Moscow Copper Co. Original

2 oz. Vodka + **1 oz. Lime Juice** + **1/4 - 1/8 tsp. Grated Ginger** + **Soda To Top** =

DIRECTIONS: Add vodka, lime juice, fresh ginger to shaker and shake. Pour into copper mug with ice and top with soda water.

Frozen Strawberry Mule

Moscow Copper Co. Original

= **1 oz. Lime Juice** + **1 Cup Frozen Strawberries** + **1/4 - 1/8 tsp. Grated Ginger** + **Ginger Beer To Top** + **2 oz. Vodka**

DIRECTIONS: Blend frozen strawberries, vodka, grated ginger and lime juice. Pour into copper mug and top with a floater of ginger beer. Garnish with lime and strawberry.

Citrus Mule

Moscow Copper Co. Original

2 oz. Vodka + 2 oz. Freshly Squeezed Orange Juice + 1 oz. Lemon Juice + Ginger Beer To Top =

DIRECTIONS: Add vodka, juiced orange and lemon to copper mug with ice. Top with ginger beer. Stir.

Watermelon Mule

Moscow Copper Co. Original

= Jalapeño + 1 oz. Lime Juice + Handful of Seedless Watermelon + Ginger Beer To Top + 2 oz. Vodka

DIRECTIONS: Pour vodka, watermelon, and jalapeño into copper mug and muddle. Add ice and top with ginger beer. Garnish with watermelon.

Mini Mules

With our two ounce mini mule mugs on hand, crafting a batch of flavorful mulestyle shots is quick, easy and fun. Here are three of our favorite mini mule recipes:

The Morning Mule
Start your day with this non-alcoholic mini mule. Featuring anti-inflammatory turmeric and ginger, healing Manuka honey and vitamin C-packed orange juice, this is a pint-sized shot of health!

Mini Marys
A full Bloody Mary is like a meal in a glass, but these petite versions are bursting with that same garden fresh tomato flavor with a hint of heat.

Hot Shot
A touch of heat and a dash of sweet, plus the warmth of ginger and turmeric, a splash of lemon juice and a shot of your favorite vodka, this miniature cocktail is spicy, zesty and utterly delightful.

The Morning Mule

HEALTHY IMMUNITY BOOSTING GINGER SHOT (NON-ALCOHOLIC)

MANUKA HONEY
2 Tablespoons

MINI MULE
2 oz. Mini Mugs

ORANGES
1/2 cup of freshly squeezed orange juice, pulp removed if desired

GINGER
1/2-inch piece ginger, grated

TURMERIC
1/2-inch fresh turmeric, grated (or pinch of ground turmeric)

DIRECTIONS:
Whisk all the ingredients in a small pitcher until combined. Pour into your Mini Mules and enjoy. Now go **MULE THE WORLD!**

Mini Marys

Moscow Copper Co. Original

1 1/2 oz.
Preservation Co.
All-Natural
Bloody Mary Mix

1/2 oz.
Vodka

Squeeze Wedge
Lime

1/4 - 1/8 tsp.
Grated Ginger

DIRECTIONS: Pour Preservation Co. Bloody Mary mix, vodka and lime to mini mule. Top with freshly grated ginger. Cheers!

Hot Shot

Moscow Copper Co. Original

Lemon

Cayenne
Pepper

Turmeric

Agave
Syrup

Ginger Beer
To Top

1/2 oz.
Vodka

DIRECTIONS: Add a pinch of cayenne pepper and turmeric to mini mule mug. Pour in vodka, a squeeze of agave syrup and lemon. Top with ginger beer.

The Copper Card...
Your Passport To The Mulehead Nation

The moment you become a Copper Card holder, you're granted access to a new set of rules.

The Copper Card was developed as a great alternative to handing over your driver's license or a credit card to bartenders simply in order to enjoy your favorite beverage in the vessel in which it should rightfully be served.

Our founder, JJ Resnick, realized that many bars had a big problem on their hands. Copper mugs can be expensive, and after serving the increasingly popular Moscow Mule cocktail in its traditional copper mug, many bars were ending the night a few mugs short. They couldn't afford to continue losing their copper mugs to folks with sticky fingers and an eye for the finer things.

To solve this epidemic, JJ Resnick came up with the Copper Card program. Patrons who become Copper Card holders will always have access to an authentic Moscow Copper Co. mug in which to enjoy their Moscow Mules.

Initially, membership has been limited to a select few Muleheads invited during the launch phase of the program. However, as the program expands, the Copper Card will become even more of a rewards and loyalty card, and will eventually change the way people experience their favorite watering holes.

Some of the membership perks include:

*20% off ALL original Moscow Copper Co. products
*An original mug Moscow Copper Co. mug will always be waiting for you at all Copper Card approved establishments worldwide

To join the Mulehead Nation and receive your Copper Card, visit CopperCardUsa.com

IT'S SCIENCE TIME!

Let's dive into the real science of why Moscow Copper Co. mugs - which are constructed of pure copper - are your best option for a true mule experience.

As a reminder, we are looking to answer the following three questions as we headed into the experiments.

1. Does the copper vessel decrease the temperature of the cocktail and does it keep it colder longer?

2. Does copper influence the taste of the cocktail?

3. Scientifically, how does the copper vessel contribute to the overall drinking experience?

TEMPERATURE

Some of the reasons why copper is so cool (pun intended) are straightforward, while others require a deeper dive.

Let's take a crash course on the principles of heat transfer.

First, the second law of thermodynamics essentially states that heat flows from an object of higher temperature to an object of lower temperature. In other words, heat moves from hot to cold.

Second, there are three types of heat transfer: Conduction, Convection, and Radiation.

- Conduction generally happens in solids or where fluids are not moving.

- Convection happens more often with fluids in motion (liquids or gases).

- Radiation occurs wherever radiant energy is able to travel.

You can witness all three around a campfire. If you put a metal poker in the fire, you may end up feeling the heat in the handle – that's conduction. If you put your hands above the fire and feel energy moving upward carrying ashes with it – that's convection. If you are sitting next to the fire and feel the heat energy on your face – that's radiant heat, which travels by electromagnetic waves across space.

Back to our copper mug…

First and foremost, copper is an incredible thermal conductor. Essentially this means that the mug will very quickly reach a temperature equilibrium with whatever fluid is poured inside. When the ice is dropped into the mug and the vodka is splashed in, the heat from the room temperate mug rushes into the fluid.

Moscow Copper Co. has taken special care to create a very light mug, which means it has less thermal mass — or copper mass that holds heat.

This makes the transfer of heat from the mug to the beverage very quick. Less conductive vessels, such as a cocktail glass are generally much heavier (more thermal mass) and they have less conductivity, which means that the vessel itself will be transferring much more heat energy into your beverage than the copper mug, and it will take a bit longer.

The copper mug lets your beverage get colder faster, transferring less heat into the beverage, enabling the beverage to reach its lowest possible temperature — which turns out to be one of the key contributors to the chemistry of the cocktail. But patience, we'll get to that in a moment.

In our tests, we repeatedly showed that not only does the copper mug get the drink colder, as well as colder faster, it also keeps the drink cooler longer. See the graph – science!

But wait, doesn't that seem counterintuitive? Wouldn't copper just take the heat from the air around you and heat up your mule? Not exactly. Remember the three methods of heat transfer? Now we get to see another awesome property of copper in action - emissivity. And we get to tip our hat to German physicist Gustav Kirchho and his Law of Thermal Radiation.

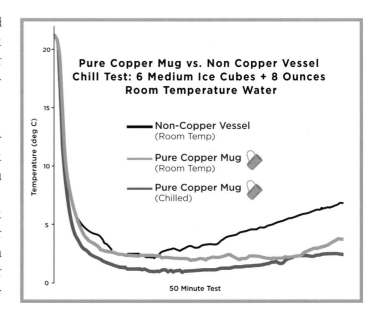

Pure Copper Mug vs. Non Copper Vessel
Chill Test: 6 Medium Ice Cubes + 8 Ounces
Room Temperature Water

Non-Copper Vessel (Room Temp)

Pure Copper Mug (Room Temp)

Pure Copper Mug (Chilled)

50 Minute Test

Quite simply, in order for radiant heat transfer to take place, it needs to be able to be absorbed by that material. In our situation, we can allow emissivity values to be representative of absorptivity values. For a glass vessel, emissivity is around .93 (where 1 is the max, also known as a Black Body) and it absorbs lots of thermal radiation. On the other hand, copper has an emissivity of .05, so you'll have a pretty hard time heating up a well-shined copper mug through radiant energy transfer. The glass or ceramic vessel will absorb radiant heat while the copper mug will reflect it. It's almost like wearing a black T-shirt versus a white T-shirt out in the direct sun.

But what about the heat from your hand or the table? Good question! That could be an issue — but a well-designed copper mug will have a large but thin handle to hold the drink. Use that handle and you'll keep your drink colder, longer. Also using a coaster will protect the bottom of the cup from a hot table on a hot day. Cork accomplishes this perfectly — it's not just for catching condensation!

These very unique properties of high thermal conductivity and very low emissivity ensure you'll have the coldest possible beverage while keeping it cooler for longer. Copper for the win.

THE INDIVIDUAL COMPONENTS

Let's jump into the science of the liquid ingredients through pH levels and electrical conductivity — pH is a logarithmic measure of the hydrogen ion concentration in an aqueous solution. Why are hydrogen ion concentrations in a liquid important? The concentration is a measure of how acidic or basic a substance is.

The pH scale ranges from 0 to 14, where pH 7 is neutral. Acids are those with a pH of less than 7 and Bases are substances above 7.

Okay, onward to electrical conductivity and Total Dissolved Solids or TDS.

TDS is a measure of negative ions (anions) and positively charged ions (cations) present in a solution. These ions may include calcium, sodium, magnesium, phosphate — the list goes on and on. It's measured in Parts Per Million (ppm). TDS has a close connection with electrical conductivity (measured in Siemens per meter [S/m]). Generally, the more ions present in a solution, the higher the electrical conductivity. In other words, high TDS usually means higher electrical conductivity

Back to our Moscow Mule. The ingredient list is short but powerful — ice, vodka, ginger beer, and lime.

Ginger beer contains various salts, vitamins, minerals, and compounds, like potassium and some naturally occurring sulfur based compounds. These tend to contribute to the increased electrical conductivity found across ginger beers. The higher the number, the more dissolved stuff in there.

Limes are a wonder of nature. Not only do they bring the acidic punch to the beverage, but also minerals and ions of calcium, iron, magnesium, phosphorous, potassium, and even some naturally-occurring copper. Low pH and high conductivity — thank you limes!

A quick digression on the power of lime — as the lime is stirred into the drink, copper citrate forms, and with the iron from the lime, produces a mild flavor that masks metallic tones, potentially from the ginger beer or the ice, hence enhancing the overall flavor of the mule.

What's the pH and TDS of these ingredients? Do they differ much? Do they differ when exposed to copper vs glass or ceramic? Let's find out.

To conduct this experiment, we gathered ingredients, did a two-point calibration on a pH sensor and a TDS meter, and gathered both pure copper (Moscow Copper Co.) and non fully copper mugs.

Tap Water	pH	TDS (ppm)	%Increase
Non-Copper	8.4	344	--
Pure Copper Mug	8.4	359	4%
Vodka	pH	TDS (ppm)	%Increase
Non-Copper	7.3	2	--
Pure Copper Mug	7.3	4	100%
Q Ginger Beer	pH	TDS (ppm)	%Increase
Non-Copper	3	245	--
Pure Copper Mug	3	270	10%
Limes	pH	TDS (ppm)	%Increase
Non-Copper	2.3	2120	--
Pure Copper Mug	2.3	2210	4%

Why we tested this:

1. Get an idea of pH and TDS (which relates to electrical conductivity) for the various Moscow Mule ingredients.

2. To see if there was any difference between the liquid in a non copper mug versus a pure copper mug.

3. To see if we notice any observations based on taste.

The takeaway:

Not all ingredients are created equal. Copper does add to the electrical conductivity of the drink, so we know that a minuscule amount of copper does interact with the ingredients of the cocktail. Is this tiny amount of copper interaction safe you may ask? Let's put it this way. To reach the EPA recommended max 1.3 mg/L MCL (max allowable concentration limit) of copper consumption, you would have to consume many many millions of Moscow Mules. We calculated a mule from a copper mug to be 0.00000000003 mg/L after utilizing data from our TDS test and crunching the numbers.

BRINGING IT ALL TOGETHER

It's time to mix it all together. Let's recap the journey thus far.

- Copper does help our Moscow Mule get cooler quicker, stay cooler longer, all while reaching a lower temperature than it would in non copper and other cocktail vessels, such as a glass.

- There's quite a lot going on in each of the individual ingredients of the Moscow Mule – from pH to TDS to minerals and differences across the particular brands and varieties of the ingredients.

- We've seen there is indeed a slight increase in TDS and electrical conductivity from the copper mug, so we can venture that a small amount of copper from the mug will interact with our ingredients. This comes into play in a number of ways. But, interestingly, there are a few people who are more sensitive to electrical changes across their body. If you are one of the few, you may even get a little electric tingle as your mouth closes the circuit across the cup to your hand with that first sip. This is a very unique characteristic of a copper mug, as glass and ceramic are insulators of electrical current.

So how does all of this make a Moscow Mule in a copper mug the best? Can we learn anything about the taste of beverage or the fizziness from a cocktail mixing experiment?

We set up one final experiment to explore the change in pH, in Electrical Conductivity (EC), in concentration of Dissolved Oxygen (DO) and in Oxidation Reduction Potential (ORP), as we mixed the drink together. This was a 30 minute test, allowing the sensors to transition the measurement from one addition to another. After multi-point sensor calibration, the mixing test was conducted on both copper mugs and glass/ceramic vessels. What did we learn? *Well first, it's time for another science lesson!*

By now, we know a bit about pH and EC, but what about the new guys – Dissolved Oxygen and Oxidation Reduction Potential? And how do they help? Dissolved Oxygen (DO), measured in milligram/L, is a measure of how much oxygen is dissolved into a solution. In this situation, Dissolved Oxygen and Dissolved Carbon Dioxide will have similar trends, so we will infer carbon dioxide (carbonation) behavior from the DO sensor.

Oxidation Reduction Potential (ORP), measured in millivolts, refers to the tendency of a chemical substance to oxidize or reduce another substance. The higher the measure of ORP, the higher the oxidative property – meaning it steals electrons.

As the ORP reading becomes a negative value, this represents a reduction, or the gaining of electrons. This is what is considered an antioxidant.

Since copper is naturally an antioxidant, the ORP sensor was included in the testing as an exploratory measurement.

Let's look at the charts from the experiment!

As expected, the electrical conductivity was slightly higher in the copper mug, likely due to interactions between the copper and the ingredients. The pH didn't change between the two, because, well, it shouldn't have, so this was good to confirm. ORP did show a small change in value, which is also likely

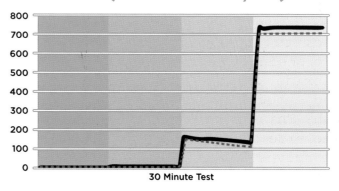

EC (microSiemens/cm)

30 Minute Test

——— Pure Copper Mug   - - - - - - Non-Copper Vessel

pH

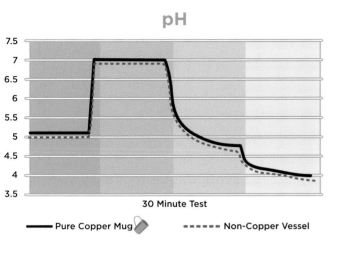

30 Minute Test

—— Pure Copper Mug ⊷   ------ Non-Copper Vessel

due to an interaction between the copper mug and the beverage.

We know now that the addition of copper contributes to the enhanced experience, and without going too deep into the chemistry – the interactions with the salts, vitamins, and minerals in the ingredients chemically cause an increase in carbonation amongst other exciting things. When it comes to carbonation, the DO sensor provides an incredible insight. What's so amazing? Quite simply, the fizziness! The carbonation in the ginger beer is what provides the bubbly fizz.

At the time of bottling, ginger beer is supersaturated with carbon dioxide gas. This is where we hope that the brand of ginger beer you choose was carbonated at the lowest temperature possible. The lower the temperature, the more soluble, or dissolvable, the carbon dioxide is.

Lower carbonation temperature means a larger carbonation density in your drink, which in turn means more opportunity for bubbles. Keep that in mind.

When the ginger beer bottle is first opened it starts to outgas due to a change in pressure. But those bubbles seem to appear from nowhere! What you are seeing is actually dissolved carbon dioxide going through a phase change and outgassing as bubbles. Pretty cool huh? This is referred to as nucleation.

ORP (millivolts)

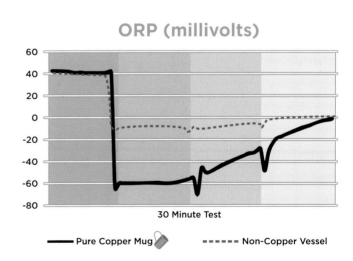

30 Minute Test

—— Pure Copper Mug ⊷   ------ Non-Copper Vessel

The size of the bubbles and the rate of bubble production depends on how much dissolved CO2 is in the liquid to start with, the temperature of the beverage (this changes the solubility of the gas), and the availability of nucleation sites — little sites that promote the formation of bubbles. [Ever notice the bubbles forming in a pot of water about to boil?] Those bubbles are forming at nucleation/cavitation sites, or rough spots on the pot's surface. It's almost the same principle at work here.

In an iced beverage, the jagged ice provides wonderful nucleation sites and promotes more active bubble formation. In a Moscow Mule, the squeezed lime contributes additional nucleation sites.

You may have noticed in cold, carbonated beverages where ice is not used, say beer or champagne, some glasses have etchings on the inside walls of the glass or on the inside bottom surface. These are there to provide nucleation sites that will increase the rate of outgassing, giving you more aroma as the bubbles carry the scent of the beverage to your nose.

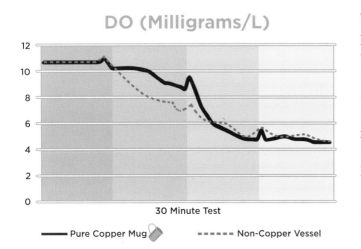

DO (Milligrams/L)

30 Minute Test

—— Pure Copper Mug   ------ Non-Copper Vessel

We now know that a Moscow Mule in copper is colder than in a regular glass, which means that at the coldest point, there is the most potential to have a fizzy sensation. And when the beverage hits your warm mouth, there is a massive and rapid degassing of CO_2 as a function of temperature change when beverage meets lips. This also increases the aroma of the beverage more than a regular glass would. You can see this in the DO graph – more area under the curve for longer means more opportunity for bubbling, fizzing fun in comparison to a regular glass. Copper wins again – from the temperature advantage to the chemical reactions with the copper – teamwork makes the Moscow Mule carbonation dream work!

And here we conclude — all the components have now been brought together with increased carbonation, and that new sweet, strange copper salt flavor that masks any, albeit rare, imperfections. As you bring the drink to your lips a wonderful aroma is unleashed. As the cup makes contact with your mouth, heat rushes from your lips into the copper, and there may even be a small jolt – the voltage from the human body meeting the fully conductive path from drink to cup to hand – which completes the full Moscow Mule experience, only possible via a 100% pure copper mug such as the Moscow Copper Co. mugs.

SO WHAT DID WE TAKE AWAY?

- If you're reaching for copper, go with the real deal pure copper mugs like Moscow Copper Co. in this case.

- Ingredients matter — go for quality and the flavors you love. It's worth it.

- Hold the mug by the handle. Use a coaster to insulate from the heat of the table — and to catch the condensation.

- Avoid using a straw — part of the experience is feeling the cooling sensation on your lips, and, just perhaps, that slight electric jolt.

- We disliked ginger beers with a lot of added sugars and other fillers — these had the most TDS and a higher pH compared to quality brands such as Q or Fever-Tree.

- Embrace the fizz, take in the scents, it's highest in those first few sips — again — no straws.

But really, science does most of the work for you — so sit back, relax, and enjoy your Moscow Mule!

Acknowledgements

It's finished! Publishing my first book has been such an incredibly humbling experience. I knew it was going to be a difficult feat, but the number of sleepless nights far exceeded my expectations. If it weren't for the incredible team I have behind me, this book would never have seen the light of day.

I'd like to start by thanking my Great Grandma, Sophie Berezinski for creating the Moscow Mule 75 years ago and giving me a blank canvas to work with. Many thanks to my entire family, especially Mom and Dad for always keeping Grandma Sophie's legacy alive. To my amazing team of designers, writers, editors, contributors, and especially my wife Candy Sue Resnick. She continues to tell me I can do anything I put my mind to and encourages me to fulfill all of my dreams. Thank you for always believing in me!

THANKS...

Tales of the Cocktail
Cheers to TOTC for deeming our 75th Anniversary the "Year of the Mule" and running such a great cocktail competition this year which inspired and compelled us to work with some of the best mixologists around the world.

Participating Bartenders
To all of the bartenders and master mixologists involved, your ingenious concoctions and spins on the classic really makes this project special and truly unique. We salute and thank you!

Juan Orozco
Juan is our Art Director and the first person I told about the book. I came to him just like I do every week with another "idea" and he listened, then even began designing concepts for the book right away which made it possible for me to go full speed ahead. I am so grateful for your clear passion for this project.

Matt Knapp
My go-to point person on the book for the last 6 months! Matt has been instrumental communicating with the team, all the bartenders and those involved to ensure the book was completed on time. Thanks for also putting your everything into this project and being there at 3am making edits and discussing new ideas, which we had plenty of. Do you ever sleep? Cheers my friend!

Paola Martin

Although Paola is new to the team this year, she has been instrumental in creating this book that we are all so incredibly proud of. Being the lead designer, she too worked around the clock finessing every single detail. Paola is also responsible for the whimsical recipe illustrations you see throughout the book. You're a rockstar!

Jo Abbie

For being the best Copy Editor I've ever worked with. No matter how frustrating the project became at times it was always calming and a pleasure hearing your Australian accent, so thanks for that!

Daniela Sylvia

For your help finishing the book before Thanksgiving. I'll never forget how you jumped out of a burning truck on the freeway for me and the book. That's true dedication if I've ever seen it.

Brandon Larson

For spending countless hours in the lab testing and then verifying the results surrounding the true benefits of the copper mug. He warned us from the start that he would have to publish all the results of the copper tests he conducted because his reputation and future were on the line which we completely understood. We knew there was a chance that his findings could ruin the symbolism and popularity of the Moscow Mule being served in the original copper mug forever...but it was a chance we also knew had to be taken. We now can definitively prove all the skeptics wrong, so thanks Brandon!

*Thanks to the rest of the Mule Team at our headquarters in Santa Barbara, our new team in Vegas, **Dot Dot**, and all the others around the world. I'm so lucky to have an amazing team. Thank you all for your dedication!*

Glossary of Bartending Terms

An A-Z of Bar Talk

Sometimes the snippets of conversation heard between bartenders over the din of cocktail shaking and ice crushing can be almost inexplicable. Here's a handy cheat sheet of some of the most commonly used and heard terms.

ABV: Alcohol by volume. And no, we're not talking about the volume of music being played inside the local bar. This term refers to the standard measure of how much alcohol is contained in a given volume of an alcoholic beverage, expressed as a percentage.

Aperitif: A cocktail served before dinner, to stimulate the appetite.

Back: A bartending term for an iced glass of water or other (usually) alcohol-free beverage served in addition to the cocktail or mixed drink being ordered. For example, "Moscow Mule with a water back, please bartender." Or a commonly heard request in many bars is "A shot of tequila with a beer back."

Behind the stick: If you hear any bartender refer to working, "behind the stick" it has nothing to do with the transmission of their car, and everything to do with them doing what generally they enjoy the most — mixing drinks behind the bar.

Bitters: While many bars used to hold one lonely-looking bottle of Angostura brand bitters, the recent cocktail renaissance means that many home bars now feature an array of different flavored bitters. Bitters are essentially aromatic, herbal compounds that are primarily bitter to the taste. The three most popular types of bitters in mixology are typically Angostura Bitters from Trinidad, Peychaud's Bitters from New Orleans and orange bitters, but today there are myriad flavors and artisanal varieties available.

Buck/Mule: The terms mule and buck are often used interchangeably. The difference? The Buck was the name historically given to all drinks that featured a blend of a spirit, ginger ale/beer and citrus. As all Muleheads know, when vodka was introduced into the American market, the Moscow Mule was created and introduced — Mule being a clever play on Buck.

Build: To pour the ingredients directly into the mixing or serving glass — or in this case, copper mug!

Chaser: A drink, often times a mixer, consumed immediately after a straight shot of liquor.

Collins: A tall, cylindrical glass, the Collins is narrower and taller than a Highball glass. It takes its name from and thus is frequently used to serve the Tom Collins, a popular drink consisting of gin, lemon juice, sugar, and carbonated water. The other members of the Collins family of cocktails include the John (replace gin with bourbon), Joe (replace gin with Scotch and soda water with cola), Juan (replace gin with tequila), and Ivan (replace gin with vodka).

Daisy: The name often given to any oversized drink of the sour type, usually made with rum or gin. It is served over crushed ice with a straw, and sweetened with a fruit syrup.

Dash: The small amount that flows when a bottle is quickly inverted once.

Digestif: A cocktail served after dinner, to aid digestion.

Dirty: The term most often used to denote the addition of a small amount of olive brine into a martini. We're not sure if a Dirty Mule exists, but we welcome any suggestions.

Dirty dump: A term used by some bartenders when the contents of the shaker - such as citrus fruit or fresh herbs — are added into the drinking vessel along with the alcohol. A classic shaken cocktail that uses a "dirty dump" is the mojito. Down: Term used to describe drinks that are served in an old fashioned or stemless glass with ice, "down" on the bar.

Double: "Bartender, make it a double," of course means the drinker is requesting two shots instead of the usual one.

Dry: Dry cocktails, typically gin or vodka martinis, are mixed with little (or no) vermouth.

Effervescent: Any liquid that characteristically is giving off bubbles or fizzy in nature. Also used to describe vivacious and enthusiastic personalities, such as our very own Grandma Sophie Berezinski!

Float: A mixology term for a product that is poured on top of a drink; often done enhance presentation. The floated product is frequently the heaviest ingredient in the recipe, and often darker in color than the remainder of the cocktail.

Finger: Old-timey term from when patrons used the width of a bartender's finger denote how much whiskey, or liquor, they desired in their glass.

Fizz: A fizz is a mixed drink variation of the sours family of cocktail. Its defining features are a spirit – often gin – flavored with an acidic juice, such as lemon or lime, and topped off with carbonated water.

Grog: A rum-based beverage with water, fruit juice and sugar, commonly served a large mug with a handle, for easy swigging.

Highball: A type of glass tumbler that is taller than an Old Fashioned glass, but shorter and wider than a Collins glass. The Highball glass gets is name from a family of mixed alcoholic drinks that are composed of an alcoholic base spirit an a larger proportion of a non-alcoholic mixer. Popular Highball drinks include the Scotch and soda or the gin and tonic.

Iced: A mixology term used in drink recipes to denote any glass involved in the preparation of a drink that needs to be filled with ice.

Jigger: A liquid measurement equaling 1 ½ ounces. The jigger also is the term often used to describe the conical handheld measuring device that features a 1 ½ shot on one side and a 1 ounce shot on the other.

Julep: A style of cocktails that hails from the American south, usually consisting bourbon, mint, sugar and crushed ice.

Keg: A wooden barrel used to brew beer, and famously, the ginger beer that is o of the key ingredients in any Moscow Mule.

...ueur: A liqueur is an alcoholic beverage made from a distilled spirit that has ...n flavored with fruit, cream, herbs, spices, flowers or nuts, and usually bottled ...n added sugar or other sweetener. Popular examples include absinthe, amaret-...Campari, Cointreau and Fernet Branca.

...ing glass or cup: A large glass with measurements marked on the side.

...ddle: To gently mash ingredients, such as bitters-soaked sugar cubes, fruit or ...h herbs, to release essential oils for aroma and flavor. Muddling is typically ...d in the preparation of mojitos, caipirinhas, old fashioneds and other cocktails ...g fresh ingredients. Also denotes when you've had one too many and get a bit ...ddled" and forget what drink you are mixing!

...lehead: A member of the Mulehead Nation, one who appreciates authenticity ... values the history of this fine drink that the Moscow Mule.

...t: Any liquor served undiluted in a glass without ice. Also how Clark Kent ...ers to many things that are "cool" or "great" — much to the annoyance of Lois ...e.

...Fashioned: A type of glass, also known as a lowball glass or rocks glass, ...ch is a short tumbler, often used for serving an alcoholic beverage, such as ...sky, with ice cubes. It is also used to serve certain cocktails, such as the Old ...hioned — from which it received its name.

...the rocks: A shot of liquor served over ice.

...ny: A one ounce shot of liquor.

...of: In America, proof is the term used to describe the alcohol content of any ...or: 100 proof is 50 percent alcohol by volume (ABV)

...inine: The element that gives tonic water its distinctive flavor, quinine is ...ived from the bark of a tree, and in the 1700s it was discovered that the bitter ...ing quinine could be used to prevent and treat malaria. British officers in ...ia in the early 19th century took to adding a mixture of water, sugar, lime and ... to the quinine in order to make the drink more palatable, and thus the now ...owned gin and tonic mixed drink was born.

...key: A particular style of drink, the basic Rickey features a liquor, usually gin, ...f a lime and soda water. It is sometimes sweetened, and often served with ice ...a rickey glass.

...cks: The same as "on the rocks." Rocks also refers to the short, tumbler style of ...ss also known as an Old Fashioned glass.

...rub: Like bitters, shrubs have regained popularity in the cocktail renaissance of ...ent years, and are essentially an acidulated beverage made of fruit juice, sugar, ...d other ingredients such as vinegar.

...mple syrup: A common ingredient in cocktails, simple syrup is, quite simply, ...al parts water and sugar, boiled to form a liquid and then cooled. Many of the ...ipes in this book require the use of a simple syrup. Bartenders and mixologists ...en infuse their simple syrups with other flavors, another thing you'll find in ...ny of amongst our plethora of mule recipes within this book.

Sling: Another style of drink, the Sling is a tall cocktail made with either brandy, whiskey or gin, plus lemon juice, sugar and soda water.

Sour: A short drink consisting primarily of liquor, lemon or lime juice and sugar.

Straight up: A preparation technique in which drink ingredients are poured into an iced mixing glass and either stirred with a bar spoon or vigorously shaken by hand, then strained of the ice into a chilled cocktail glass. See also "Up."
Tiki: A style of tropical cocktail, also known by many as "boat drinks", usually involving rum, pineapple or other tropical fruit juices, and a colorful paper umbrella.

Tin: What many bartenders call the bottom portion of the cocktail shaker.

Toddy: A warm boozy drink, usually featuring hot water and a brown liquor such as whiskey or brandy, plus the addition of sweetener (sugar or honey) and spices (cinnamon is popular).

Twist: The pretty swirl of citrus peel that often adorns cocktails, such as a martini.

Up: A drink served in a stemmed cocktail glass, such as a coupe or a martini glass, without ice, having been chilled in a cocktail shaker prior to being poured into the stemmed glass.

Virgin: A non-alcoholic version of any cocktail. To make a Virgin Mule, simply omit the vodka.

Well drink: The bar term for a mixed drink, such as a gin and tonic or a vodka soda, made using a non-specific brand of liquor.

Xanthia: The Xanthia is an old-fashioned cocktail that blends equal parts (3/4s of an ounce) of cherry brandy, gin and Yellow Chartreuse. The name is thought to have been derived from the Greek word xanthos, meaning "yellow" or "fair hair," hence the inclusion of the Yellow Chartreuse.

Yankee Punch: According to the 1957 Esquire Drink Book, the Yankee Punch is a potent punch bowl cocktail — a mixture of 2 quarts rye whiskey, 1 pint of New England rum, 6 sliced lemons, 1 sliced pineapple, 4 quarts of water, sugar to taste, and ice for serving.

Zubrówka: Better known in English as Bison Grass Vodka, this is a dry, herb-flavored vodka that is distilled from rye and bottled at 40% alcohol by volume. Its unique flavor comes from a a tincture of bison grass, which also gives the spirit its yellowish color. It is described as having woodruff, vanilla, coconut and almond notes. The name Zubrówka comes from Zubr, the Polish word for the European bison, a breed that is particularly fond of eating this grass.

Index

A

Absinthe - 148, 237
Absolut - 32, 87
Absolut Elyx - 76
Absolut Ruby Red - 28
Admiralty Blend - 114, 177
Agave Syrup - 220
Amaro Averna - 47
Amaro Montenegro - 80, 110, 160, 164
Ancho Reyes - 35, 127, 136, 139, 170
Angostura - 51, 52, 76, 101, 152, 236
Anhydrous - 97
Aylesbury Duck Vodka - 35, 40, 47, 59

B

Ballast Point - 174
Bar Keep Apple - 72
Barbancourt - 169, 173, 182, 188
Barritt - 31, 60, 127
Barrow's Intense Ginger - 63, 83, 178
Basil - 40, 98, 173
Bittercube Corazón - 98
Black Pepper - 35
Black Walnut - 105
Bluecoat - 101
Bulleit - 144, 148, 155, 163, 164

C

Cardamom - 29, 83, 177, 188, 189, 194
Carrot Juice - 147, 163, 178
Cayenne - 71, 84, 48, 220
Chai - 98
Chamomile - 75, 164
Cherry - 144
Cinnamon - 51, 102, 135, 155
Citrus - 27
Cock'n Bull - 174
Coriander - 91, 113, 120
Crème de Violette - 28
Cucumber Juice - 27
Cutler's - 106

D

Deadhead - 174
Deep Eddy grapefruit - 43
Dolin Blanc Vermouth - 87
Dolin Génépy des Alpes - 36, 98
Domaine De Canton - 47, 48
Don Julio Blanco - 135
Don Q Cristal - 177

E

Earl Grey - 105
East Imperial - 40, 143, 147
East Imperial Yuzu - 98
Egg White - 31, 103, 106
Elemekule Tiki - 155
Elijah Craig - 128, 147

F

Fever-Tree - 35, 51, 55, 63, 76, 84, 109, 110, 123, 132, 156, 163, 169, 170, 178, 181, 182, 195, 233

G

Galangal - 51, 97, 184, 190
Giffard Banane du Bresil - 131
Giffard Bigallet - 182
Giffard Ginger of the Indies - 39, 1[
Giffard Orgeat - 131
Giffard Vanille - 182, 56
Ginger - 27, 28, 31, 32, 35, 36, 39, 40, 43, 44, 48, 52, 55, 56, 59, 60, 63, 64, 67, 68, 71, 72, 73, 75, 76, 79, 80, 83, 84, 87, 88, 91, 93, 97, 98, 101, 10[, 105, 106, 109, 110, 113, 114, 119, 12[, 123, 124, 127, 128, 131, 132, 135, 13[, 139, 143, 144, 147, 148, 151, 152, 15[, 156, 159, 160, 163, 164, 169, 170, 17[, 174, 177, 178, 181
Ginger Syrup - 27, 35, 87, 91, 97, 98[, 102, 124, 139, 148, 169, 182
Gosling's - 43, 44, 52, 75, 114, 135
Grand Marnier - 52
Granny Smith - 72
Grey Goose - 43, 88

H

Habanero Chili - 114
Haven - 55
Hella - 127
Hellfire - 47
Hendrick's gin - 109
Herradura Reposado - 132
Hibiscus Bud - 56, 113
Hibiscus Tea - 63
Honey - 71, 128, 173, 181
Housewife's Grapefruit - 28

J

Jalapeño - 124
John D. Taylor's Velvet Falernum - 28
Jura Superstition - 143, 156

K

Kaffir - 64, 96
Kahlua - 60
Karlsson's - 60
Ketel One - 27, 48, 51, 64, 67, 72, 79, 189
Kiwi - 124

L

La Nina Primario Mezcal - 132
La Quintinye Vermouth Royal Rouge - 152
Lemongrass - 28
Leopold - 151
Lillet Blanc - 101

M

Maine Root - 157
Mango purée - 127
Miso Sugar - 88
Monin Habanero - 137
Monkey Shoulder - 159, 160
Montelobos Mezcal - 63, 120, 123, 127, 128, 131, 136, 139, 169

N

New Amsterdam - 55, 143
Noilly Prat Ambre - 132

O

Old Jamaica - 88
Orange Juice - 147

P

Peach Nectar - 67
Peychaud - 35, 59, 188, 236
Pineapple Juice - 32, 52, 182,
Pink Peppercorn - 83
Pistachio Infused - 68
POM Juice - 200
Preservation Co. Bloody Mary Mix - 220
Prosecco - 101
Punzoné Organic - 80
Pusser - 114, 177, 178, 181

Q

Q Ginger Beer - 67, 80, 128

R

Raft Hibiscus Lavender - 113
Raisin - 182
Raspberries - 80, 105
Red Bell Pepper - 147
Reyka - 31, 36, 52, 63, 75
Rhubarb - 48, 105, 114
Rittenhouse - 152

S

Sake - 27
Salt - 35, 44, 52, 169
Shiso - 27, 144
Simple Syrup - 47, 69, 76, 101, 105, 106, 136, 156, 160, 177,
Soda Water - 27, 28, 35, 44, 59, 91, 102, 113, 139
St. Germain Elderflower - 31
Stoli Blueberry - 207
Stoli Elit - 92
Stoli Ginger Beer - 199, 211
Stoli Gluten Free - 211
Stoli Original - 199, 200, 213
Stoli Peach - 202
Stone's Original Green Ginger - 144
Sugar Syrup - 36, 163

T

Tarragon-lime - 43
Tin Cup - 151
Top Hat - 64

V

Vida Mezcal - 84

W

Wasabi - 28
Watermelon - 214

Y

Yuzu - 144, 156

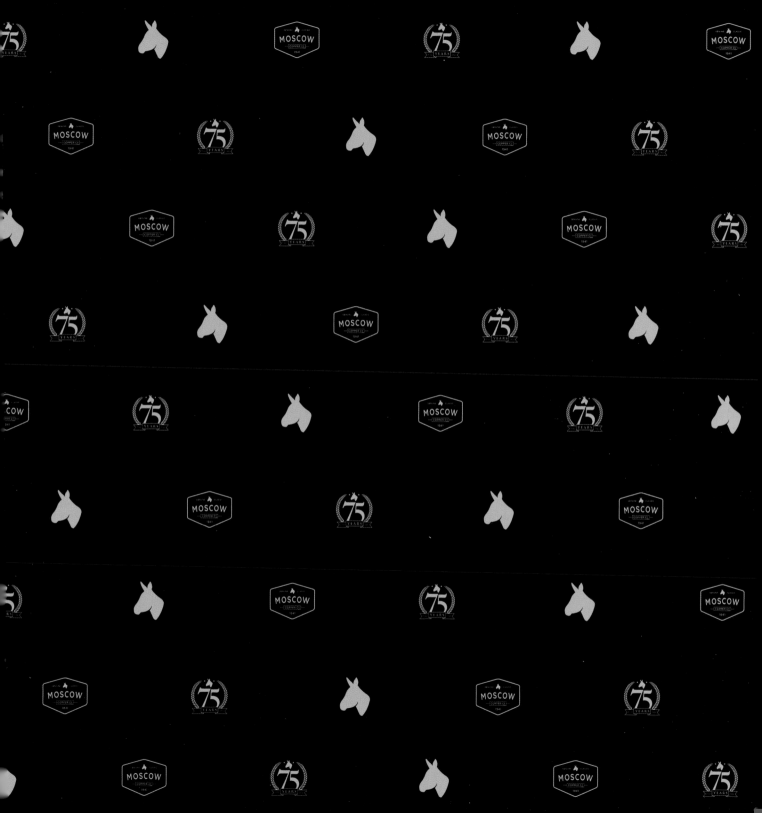

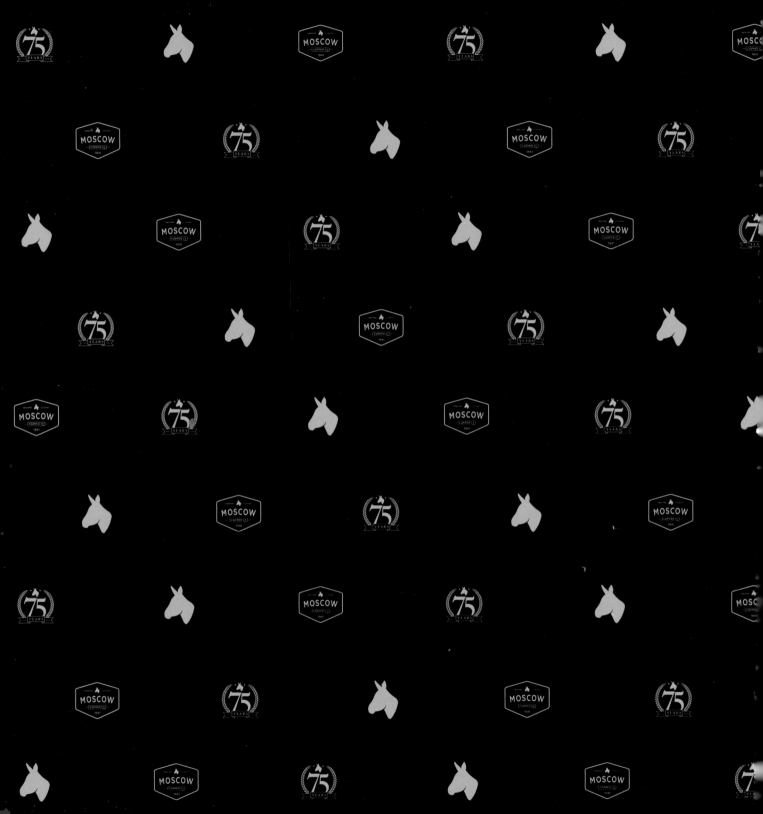